T0318707

Cambridge Elements ≡

Elements in the Philosophy of Ludwig Wittgenstein
edited by
David G. Stern
University of Iowa

READING WITTGENSTEIN'S *TRACTATUS*

Mauro Luiz Engelmann
Federal University of Minas Gerais (UFMG) and CNPq

CAMBRIDGE
UNIVERSITY PRESS

University Printing House, Cambridge CB2 8BS, United Kingdom

One Liberty Plaza, 20th Floor, New York, NY 10006, USA

477 Williamstown Road, Port Melbourne, VIC 3207, Australia

314–321, 3rd Floor, Plot 3, Splendor Forum, Jasola District Centre, New Delhi – 110025, India

103 Penang Road, #05-06/07, Visioncrest Commercial, Singapore 238467

Cambridge University Press is part of the University of Cambridge.

It furthers the University's mission by disseminating knowledge in the pursuit of education, learning, and research at the highest international levels of excellence.

www.cambridge.org
Information on this title: www.cambridge.org/9781108744409
DOI: 10.1017/9781108887892

© Mauro Luiz Engelmann 2021

First published 2021

A catalogue record for this publication is available from the British Library.

ISBN 978-1-108-74440-9 Paperback
ISSN 2632-7112 (online)
ISSN 2632-7104 (print)

Reading Wittgenstein's *Tractatus*

Elements in the Philosophy of Ludwig Wittgenstein

DOI: 10.1017/9781108887892
First published online: June 2021

Mauro Luiz Engelmann
Federal University of Minas Gerais (UFMG) and CNPq

Author for correspondence: Mauro Luiz Engelmann,
mauroengelmann@gmail.com

Abstract: This Element presents a concise and accessible view of the central arguments of Wittgenstein's *Tractatus Logico-Philosophicus*. Starting from the difficulties found in historical and current debates, drawing on the background of Russell's philosophy, and grounded in the ladder structure expressed in the numbering system of the book, this Element presents the central arguments of the *Tractatus* in three lines of thought. The first concerns the role of the so-called 'ontology' and its relationship to the method of the *Tractatus* and its logical symbolism, which displays the formal essence of language and world. The second deals with the symbolic unity of language and its role in the 'ladder structure' and explains how and why the book is not self-defeating. The third elucidates Wittgenstein's claim to have solved in essentials all philosophical problems, whose very formulation, he says, rests on misunderstandings.

Keywords: Wittgenstein, Tractatus, resolute reading, formal unity of language, ladder metaphor

ISBNs: 9781108744409 (PB), 9781108887892 (OC)
ISSNs: 2632-7112 (online), 2632-7104 (print)

Contents

1 Readings of the *Tractatus* and How to Read It

1.1 A Variety of Readings

In this section, I briefly indicate central features of the history of readings of the *Tractatus* in order to bring into perspective the current debate, which is then discussed in Sections 1.2–1.4.[1] From all this, in Section 1.5, I identify benchmarks for the correct reading.

In the first reactions to the *Tractatus* in Cambridge and Vienna, readers voiced some concerns about the nature of the sentences of the book.[2] In his introduction, Russell claimed that Wittgenstein managed to say a lot of things that, according to his own restrictions, could not be said (TLP: introduction, xxiii). What underlies Russell's concern is a fundamental interpretational problem. Wittgenstein writes that anyone who understands him recognizes his sentences as nonsense and *must* "throw away the ladder after he has climbed up it" (TLP: 6.54). This looks paradoxically self-defeating, for the very sentences of the book seem to give the argument for why they are nonsense. It seems that one must conclude paradoxically that if the sentences are true, they must be nonsense, but if they are nonsense, they cannot be true. In the Vienna Circle, sentences of the *Tractatus* were taken as preparatory elucidations that should be left behind in "pure science" (Neurath, 1931a: 52). However, Tractarian elucidations became a problem in the Circle because of their "metaphysical mood," which suggested inexpressible mysticism (Neurath, 1931b: 60). Carnap's notion of 'syntax' was used to address the problem. Allegedly, Wittgenstein's and Carnap's "syntactical sentences about the language of science" are legitimate, but elucidations related to the mystical are not (Carnap, 1934: 284, 314).

While in contact with the Vienna Circle in the late 1920s, Wittgenstein reworked some views that he presented in the *Tractatus*, and embedded them in epistemology. Difficulties concerning the logical independency of elementary propositions prompted him to take elementary propositions as descriptions of immediate experience (see RLF). He was *changing* the philosophy of the *Tractatus*.[3] However, "positivists" who were not really members of the Circle, particularly Popper and Ayer, erroneously considered that at the time of the *Tractatus* elementary propositions were Russellian descriptions of immediate experience. Against this background, "anti-positivistic" readings of the book were developed.

---

[1] Ideas of Sections 1.2–1.3 were introduced in Engelmann (2018a).
[2] For a history of interpretations of the *Tractatus*, see Biletzki (2003).
[3] See Engelmann (2013, 2017, and 2018c).

In the first book ever devoted to an exposition of the principal themes of the *Tractatus*, Anscombe correctly argued that the *Tractatus* did not specify elementary propositions as descriptions of immediate experience and that there was no epistemology there (Anscombe, 1959: 26–7).[4] At the same time, she seemed to confirm Neurath's fear of the mystical when she defended the presence of a lurking "transcendental" in the book in the form of "the mystical and the meaning of life" (Anscombe, 1959: 171). What grounded Anscombe's book was the adoption of what I would like to call a 'Fregean perspective.' The underlying idea was that, since the positivist reading had derived much of its plausibility from a Russellian epistemology, the logical background of Frege could direct the correct reading of the *Tractatus* (Anscombe, 1959: 12). As we will see below, the Fregean perspective will be influential in some readings.

After Anscombe, opposing positivist readings becomes a tradition. 'Mystical readings' got traction and substance in the 1960s with the publication of Paul Engelmann's *Memoir* (1967) and in the 1970s with Janik & Toulmin's *Wittgenstein's Vienna* (1973). The *Memoir* brought to light a series of influences on Wittgenstein, which apparently were very distant from Viennese positivism and the logicism of Frege and Russell. Tolstoy, Dostoevsky, Kraus, Loos, and Weininger were influences that supposedly demonstrated that fundamental ethical and religious views were the real point of the *Tractatus*, a hidden key to interpreting it. The conclusion was that, for Wittgenstein, what "really matters" is the existence of something that "transcends the realm of facts" (Engelmann, 1967: 97, 105). Although "logically untenable," sentences of the *Tractatus* that allegedly make that point are "valid" (Engelmann, 1967: 110).

If one adds to all this the letter that Wittgenstein wrote to Ficker telling him that the point of the *Tractatus* was ethical (Janik and Toulmin 1973: 143–4), one arrives at what Janik and Toulmin called the "central paradox" of the book: "how one is to reconcile the 'ethical' with the 'logical' Wittgenstein" (1973: 26). According to them, one has to give "primacy to the 'ethical' interpretation" (1973: 25) for two reasons: because Wittgenstein did not accept others' interpretations of his work when he was alive and because Paul Engelmann's testimony is "more authoritative" (1973: 25). However, those reasons are not satisfying. Wittgenstein explicitly disagreed only with Russell's interpretation of the *Tractatus*. By itself this does not give us a ground for the priority of an

---

[4] Anscombe's *An Introduction to Wittgenstein's Tractatus* (1959) is a landmark in Wittgenstein studies, for it presents the first monograph devoted to giving a detailed account of the *Tractatus*. However, its title is somewhat misleading, for her book is not introductory in the sense that it will help an unprepared reader find his way around. Rather, it is a sophisticated and intricate exposition of several of the insights of the *Tractatus*. For accessible introductions, see Mounce (1989) and White (2006), which are clearly introductory without losing sight of the systematic character of the *Tractatus*.

ethical interpretation, since Wittgenstein never criticized Russell for not paying attention to *that*. Moreover, Janik and Toulmin underestimate the significance of Russell's own views on ethics and mysticism (see Sections 4.3–4.4). Finally, although Paul Engelmann's testimony is important, it cannot be more authoritative than others, for he was neither a specialist in logic, nor well acquainted with the works of Frege and Russell. One might even think that the "ethical Wittgenstein" is the "logical" one (see Sections 4.1–4.5).

Nonetheless, Janik and Toulmin's interpretation opened new and important perspectives into the historical context of the *Tractatus*. They showed that cultural surroundings and philosophical debates in Vienna must be relevant, and that works of Tolstoy, Kraus, Kierkegaard, and Schopenhauer were part of Wittgenstein's background. The case of Kierkegaard and his presumed authorial strategies is particularly interesting because it will return in the "resolute reading" (Section 1.3). According to Janik and Toulmin (1973: 202), "to penetrate the heart of Wittgenstein's *arguments*" we need to "understand *him*," as is suggested by Wittgenstein himself in TLP 6.54. They think that understanding *him* means understanding the style, actions, and influences of the author of the book. For them, the style of the *Tractatus* is inspired by Kierkegaard and Kraus. Kierkegaard meant to bring his reader, by means of "indirect communication" grounded in irony, to the "threshold of knowledge, so as to permit him to cross over it by himself" (Janik and Toulmin, 1973: 159). One must paradoxically leap into the absurd in order to reach the sphere of absolute value, which is beyond the realm of facts (1973: 160–1). Reason brings one to paradox and transcending reason results in a higher truth beyond reason that is communicated indirectly. On their reading, the 'ethical' in the *Tractatus* is in the same situation. Kierkegaardian "indirect communication" is also envisaged by Janik and Toulmin as one of the ways to characterize the *Tractatus* as a work closely connected to Karl Kraus – a confessed influence on Wittgenstein. The last aphorisms of the *Tractatus* would show a "Krausian irony, for Wittgenstein considers that this [Tractarian] 'nonsense' is anything but *unimportant*" (Janik and Toulmin, 1973: 199). The "paradoxical and self-defeating" character of the book is "less astonishing" (1973: 199), they argue, if we understand that aphorisms, following a Krausian interpretation, are never strictly true. I will evaluate this 'authorial conspiracy' reading indirectly in my discussion of the resolute reading, which assumes something similar (Section 1.3).

A second anti-positivist trend after Anscombe's book is the metaphysical reading: the view that a necessary underlying structure of reality determines the structure of language. In its weaker version, as in Black (1966), the 'ontology' "plays an essential part in Wittgenstein's thought," particularly because the "necessary feature" of independence of atomic facts grounds an inference to a feature of the "essence of language," namely the logical independence of elementary (atomic) propositions (1966: 35). In Black's *Tractatus*, logic is important because "it leads to metaphysics" (1966: 4).

Black grounds such a view in Wittgenstein's remark in *Notes on Logic*: "[Philosophy] consists of logic and metaphysics, the former its basis" (NL: 93). He thinks that it means "Logic as the *basis* of metaphysics" (Black, 1966: 4). As Rhees points out, however, Wittgenstein says something different, namely that logic is the basis of philosophy, and not of metaphysics (Rhees, 1970: 24). Of course, the logical basis of philosophy might destroy metaphysics or make it dispensable (I return to this in Section 3.1–3).

Rhees, together with Winch and Ishiguro, inaugurated a "non-metaphysical" reading at the end of the 1960s. It was further developed by McGuinness, and more recently by McGinn (see Section 1.4). The reading takes logic and language as the real issues in the *Tractatus*. "We could say," argues Rhees, "that someone knows [. . .] what language is, if he has learned to speak," which includes an idea "of what it makes sense to ask, or what it makes sense to say" (Rhees, 1970: 47).[5] So the *Tractatus* presents us with its notions of logic and sense, but we already know them implicitly in our linguistic practices. What Tractarian logical analysis leads one to "is just what ordinary propositions show. Only it is made clearer" (Rhees, 1970: 10). In order to understand the book, Rhees claims, one must pay particular attention to "form and the symbolism" (1970: 37). The apparently 'ontological' beginning, thus, does not express metaphysical truths, but the idea that "it would have no sense at all to speak of logical propositions unless there were empirical propositions" (Rhees, 1970: 23). As the context principle makes clear (TLP: 3.3), "apart from language" a proposition that describes states of affairs "would not be a proposition" (Rhees, 1970: 27). What gives sense to the idea of correspondence is not state of affairs or objects as meanings of names, but "the picturing or projection in a proposition" (TLP: 4.0141). When I am projecting, "I am committed to the signs I use and the ways I combine them – by the general rule, the syntax of the language" (Rhees, 1970: 27–8). Although there are gaps in Rhees' insights, in particular the lack of a real explanation of the role of the 'ontology,' they must be taken seriously by any reader of the *Tractatus*.

Ishiguro brought a more solid basis to the non-metaphysical reading. She argued that realist readings misleadingly presuppose that "the meaning of a name can be secured independently of its use in propositions" (Ishiguro, 1969: 20). Such readings assumed a Russellian perspective in which meaning

---

[5] Rhees (1970) is a collection of previously published papers.

is given independently of the context of a proposition, but the context principle tells us otherwise: "Only propositions have sense; only in the nexus of a proposition does a name have meaning" (TLP 3.3). A name can only refer to a fixed object if it has a "fixed use," and the use of a name is only fixed contextually "in a set of propositions" (Ishiguro, 1969: 21, 27, 33). So the key Tractarian view is the context principle in TLP 3.3 and 3.326–8 (Ishiguro, 1969: 22, 29, 30). The origin of the principle, she argues, is Fregean, and one must understand that it works against Russell's epistemological views on meaning.[6] On this reading, something like a "private act" of acquaintance with an object, as Russell thought was fundamental, "would not make a sound into a name of an object" (Ishiguro, 1969: 27). Thus, the talk of objects given independently of language use is useless. According to McGuinness, Ishiguro's reading indicates that the 'ontology' is rather a mythology meant to be destroyed "by its own absurdity" (McGuinness, 2002: 95). Any account of the *Tractatus* as grounded in an ontology that provides a semantical framework for the meaning of names is itself a metaphysical account rejected in the book.

Despite the work by Rhees, Ishiguro, and McGuinness, a strong version of a metaphysical reading became a standard interpretation in the 1980s in works by Malcolm (1986), Hacker (1986), and Pears (1987). All those interpretations construe Wittgenstein as presupposing a kind of Russellian epistemology.

Malcolm maintains that the meaning of names needs a "fixed use," but that what fixes use is the object named (1986: 29). According to Malcolm, a name stands for a particular object because the "name reflects the form of the object," and a form of an object "consists of the possibilities of combining with other objects in states of affairs" (1986: 29). From this he concludes that "the objects are the foundation or the theory of logical syntax of the *Tractatus*," and are " 'metaphysical entities' in the sense that their existence is deduced as a necessary presupposition of the form of the world, and of thought and language" (Malcolm, 1986: 30). The "necessary presupposition" is deeply metaphysical: any world imaginable must have the same form (the same objects) (Malcolm, 1986: 61). This is the "metaphysical underpinning" of the *Tractatus* (Malcolm, 1986: 32). However, Malcolm does not explain *how* objects miraculously determine names and fix their use. This problem will find strange solutions in other metaphysical readings (see below). On Malcolm's view, Wittgenstein was not aware of the "metaphysical character" of his conceptions (1986: 33). To say the least, this is implausible, particularly because Wittgenstein explicitly calls his sentences "nonsensical" (TLP 6.54).

---

[6] Frege's principle appears in, for instance, (1884: introduction, §60) and (1903: §97).

According to Pears, "the essential structure of our language is imposed on it by the ultimate structure of reality" (1987: 28). This structure is the "grid" of objects that constitutes "the one and only world": "at that basic level all languages have the same structure, dictated by the structure of reality" (Pears, 1987: 88). Pears' Wittgenstein defends an "uncritical realism" in which "the question, whether we contribute anything to the constitution of that world, is not even asked" (1987: 29). Like Malcolm, he assumed the unlikely view that Wittgenstein did not see the implications of his philosophy. For Pears, objects determine names because "the nature of the object *takes over and controls* the logical behavior of the name *causing* it to make sense in some sentential contexts but not in others" (1987: 88; my emphasis). This is very strange, for "superstition is the belief in the causal nexus" (TLP-OT: 5.1361). Objects "taking over" and "controlling" names is a rather magical or superstitious metaphysical view. However, Pears' formulation points to the fact that something of the sort is indeed *needed* in a metaphysical reading; otherwise, "the grid of objects" or Malcolm's "metaphysical entities" are quite useless. Realist readers need a proxy playing the role of Russell's theory of acquaintance with or without causality.

Hacker's solution consists in reading the *Tractatus* somehow more consistently than Pears and Malcolm, but making it extremely metaphysical, a case of "transcendental idealism coupled with empirical realism" (Hacker, 1986: 63). Underlying the *Tractatus*, there is a "Doctrine of the Linguistic Soul" (Hacker, 1986: 75). For Hacker, Wittgenstein establishes the "conditions of possibility" of language by means of the picture theory of meaning. The essence of this theory, as in Malcolm, is that *kinds* of simple objects determine the combinatorial possibilities (categories) of simple names (Hacker, 1986: 20–1). "Logico-syntactical forms" of names, he thinks, mirror "the metaphysical forms of the objects they stand for," so that the "range of possible worlds" is ultimately exhausted by them (Hacker, 1986: 60). This is 'realism' (Hacker, 1986: 63). The "linguistic soul" comes in because meanings are taken from simple objects and "injected" into simple names by 'projection,' a task of the transcendental subject. Thus, we get 'transcendental idealism' by means of a "metalinguistic soul" that creates language (Hacker, 1986: 100). For Hacker, meaning injection must be 'transcendental,' because neither an ordinary fact connected with any causal relation nor an ordinary true thought can establish it, for both options would bring an element of contingency into the theory (as in Pears' version of realism). So he thinks that there is "a mental act (albeit of a transcendental self, not the self studied by psychology) that injects meaning or significance into signs, whether in thought or in language" (Hacker, 1986: 75). As an 'injection,' a *non*-normative relation between indefinable names and objects establishes meaning (Hacker, 1986: 73).

It seems that Hacker would like to attribute Russell's theory of acquaintance to the *Tractatus*, but ends up attributing a proxy "transcendental" acquaintance, which is more doubtful and metaphysical than Russell's acquaintance theory itself. All these metaphysical views are presumably "ineffable metaphysical necessities" that are communicated by means of "illuminating nonsense" (Hacker, 1986: 54, 18).

Hacker understands that if the "metaphysical combinatorial possibilities" of objects determine the combinatorial possibilities of names, and thus nonsense is the violation of those possibilities, one must assume that there are "ontological types" of objects (1986: 18–20). Against the most obvious suggestion that this would imply a Wittgensteinian theory of types, he argues that Wittgenstein can abandon Russell's theory of types because "if we know the meaning of a symbol, we already know its combinatorial possibilities" (Hacker, 1986: 21). As we saw, 'knowing' is a proxy for "transcendental" acquaintance.

Metaphysical readings disrupt a fundamental guiding line of the *Tractatus*: "logic must take care of itself" (NB: 2; TLP: 5.47). "Necessity *de re*" grounded in types or kinds of objects violates the autonomy of logic that Wittgenstein considered fundamental.[7] The problem with Russell's theory of types is not that it is "metaphysically necessary" and nonsense, but that meaning ought never to play a role in logic (TLP: 3.33). Contrary to Hacker, "the whole theory of things, properties, etc. is superfluous" (NB: 2). Wittgenstein never says that mental acts of a transcendental subject inject meaning into names through projection. Moreover, contra Hacker, projection is normative, grounded in general rules (TLP: 4.01n).[8] As we will see in Sections 2.3–2.6, Wittgenstein had very good reason to hold that it is out of the question that logic should depend on any experience whatsoever.

However, despite Hacker's view that simple objects are determinants of combinatorial possibilities of simple names, and therefore of what supposedly counts as nonsense, his elucidation of why philosophical propositions and the propositions of the book are nonsense does not rely on that. He uses bipolarity as the ultimate criterion of sense. According to him, the nonsense written in the *Tractatus* results from the ascription of "internal properties," but this cannot be

---

[7] The expression *de re* occurs in Hacker (1999: 120), where he defends Malcolm's interpretation. For Hacker, Wittgenstein's later philosophy presents a *de dicto* view of necessity and a critique of the alleged Tractarian idea of *de re* necessity. See Engelmann (2011) for a critique of the presuppositions of such a view and Engelmann (2013) for a different interpretation of Wittgenstein's philosophical development.

[8] From now on, I use 'n' in for instance '4.01n' to refer to the group of remarks following 4.01.

done because "a proposition with a sense [. . .] must be bipolar" (Hacker, 2000: 355). This by itself shows that the role that objects are meant to play is superfluous, since they do not take part in the determination of nonsense. Moreover, since analysis is part of the application of logic (TLP: 5.557), which is absent in the *Tractatus*, if Hacker's combinatorial-realist reading was correct, Wittgenstein would not be authorized to call anything 'nonsense' in his book.

In the end, the metaphysical tradition of reading the book is simply in disagreement with the claim that the book provided us with nothing less than "the final solution of the problems" (TLP: preface) and that it was the "logical finishing [*logische Erledigung*] of philosophy" (Hänsel, 2012: 45). The *Tractatus* cannot achieve those goals as an exotic variety of metaphysics that generates new philosophical problems.

1.2 Resoluteness

Diamond (1996) was not only a wake-up call for those slumbering in metaphysical readings, but also a landmark that brought the *Tractatus* back into the focus of philosophical debate. The historical significance of her "resolute reading" lies in the fact that it offers an alternative reading that could show a way out of difficulties present in metaphysical readings. Moreover, she and other resolute readers have made fundamental contributions to many aspects of the interpretation of the *Tractatus*.[9]

However, it is not easy to unify the wide variety of resolute readings.[10] They do agree on two ideas: there is no theory of meaning and no ineffable nonsensical "truths" in the *Tractatus* (Conant and Diamond, 2004). The trouble here is that one might agree on this without agreeing with the way resolute readers try to show it – see, for instance, McGinn (2006) and Hutto (2006). Without its specificities, the reading collapses into anti-metaphysical readings.

Here I will focus mostly on Diamond and Conant, for it is the specificities of their work that has motivated and has kept the reading moving in the last decades. However, they have not yet offered a complete reading of the *Tractatus*; the reading is still programmatic (Conant and Diamond, 2004: 43). Fundamentally, their reading opposes Hacker's metaphysical reading and the mystical reading, both of which construe the book as containing nonsensical ineffable truths and a theory of meaning. Also, the resolute reading has changed

---

[9] Among many others, Conant (1993), Floyd (2001), Goldfarb (2002), Kremer (1997, 2007), Ricketts (1996, 2014), and Diamond (2019) are such contributions.

[10] For the variety of resolute readings, see McManus (2006), Hutto (2006), and Conant and Bronzo (2017).

over time. We have to consider both the earlier 'frame-context reading' and the later 'piecemeal nonsense reading,' which perhaps makes the first more precise.

According to the frame-context reading, we must take the 'frame' of the book seriously, namely the preface and the 'conclusion' (TLP: 6.53–7). The significance of the 'frame' comes from Wittgenstein's letter to von Ficker, in which he urges Ficker to look at the preface and the ending of the book, where the sense of the whole is easier to understand (Conant 2005: 45–6). For Diamond and Conant, the fundamental point of the 'conclusion' is that we should understand *him*, the author Wittgenstein, "instead of his nonsensical sentences" (Diamond, 1996: 19). Now, "understanding the author" is not understanding a Krausian author as for Janik and Toulmin (1973), but understanding the "frame," the author's directions for reading the book (Conant, 1993: 216; Diamond, 2000: 149–51). Since the preface tells us that "what lies on the other side of the limit" of language is simply nonsense, the nonsense of the book, according to TLP: 6.54, is simply nonsense as well, and not "illuminating nonsense" of the "metaphysically necessary" or "mystical" kind. The second aspect of the 'frame' consists in understanding that the author's purpose is to entice the reader with the illusion of a theory so that she eventually sees for herself that there is no theory after all (I come back to this in Section 1.3).

We have seen above that Ishiguro used the Fregean context principle to reject the attribution of realism to the *Tractatus* by claiming that the meaning of a name is identical with its logical syntactical employment.[11] Diamond develops a new use for it (Diamond, 1996: 109, 194–6). For Diamond, a traditional reader like Hacker is "irresolute" when he talks about illuminating nonsense that violates combinatorial possibilities of simple objects. This is simply not the Tractarian view of nonsense. According to her, the "Frege-Wittgenstein view of nonsense" implies that there is only one kind of nonsense (Diamond, 1996: 104). Two moves ground her view. First, she argues that Wittgenstein has a "judgment based" view of the proposition according to the Fregean context principle, and not an "object based" view like Russell (Diamond, 2019: 9; 1996: 100). Second, the Fregean context principle implies that there is only one kind of nonsense. This, she argues, is manifest in the following remark by Wittgenstein: " 'Socrates is identical' means nothing because we have failed to make an arbitrary determination, and not because the symbol, in itself, would be illegitimate" (TLP 5.473). Since words only have meaning (are symbols) in context, there is no such thing as a nonsensical proposition in itself and, therefore, there is no restriction for the combination of names (violation of combinatorial possibilities) either. Words have meanings as long as *we*

---

[11] In Section 2, we will see the Russellian contextual view.

determine the contribution that they make to the sense of the whole proposition. Thus, if something that looks like a proposition is in fact nonsense, then it has no sense and, consequently, its constituent parts have no meaning at all (they are not symbols). Thus, "words do not have meaning" boils down to the fact that *we* have failed to give them meaning, although we could have done so (TLP: 5.473). According to Diamond and Conant, from the logical point of view of the *Tractatus* "objects are simple" is as nonsensical as gibberish. For Diamond and Conant, we can follow the nonsensical sentences of the *Tractatus* only 'imaginatively' as somehow expressions of Wittgenstein's intention. They are "transitional remarks" intended to show ultimately that they are, indeed, simply nonsense (Diamond, 2000).

On this reading, sentences TLP 3.3 and 5.473 must help us determine the nonsensicality of sentences. However, they are not part of what Diamond called the "frame" originally. Conant's answer to this problem is that remarks outside the original "frame" might *function as* frame elucidations according to their "role within the work" (Conant, 2000: 100). This broader sense of frame implies two difficult tasks: how to decide which remarks have such a role and how to decide who decides it. The enlargement of the 'frame' introduces precluded exceptions. Wittgenstein does not say in the 'frame' (understood in its original or in its broader sense) that only some of his sentences are nonsense. He simply says, without exceptions, that his sentences elucidate in the same way and are nonsense (TLP: 6.54). This takes away some of the credibility of the reading, for the original frame story has been taken only "as seriously as possible" (Conant and Bronzo, 2017: 176), but not seriously enough in light of the original standards of resoluteness.

Moreover, although Wittgenstein indeed says in his letter to Ficker that the sense or point of the *Tractatus* is expressed in the preface and ending, he does not say that the 'ending' corresponds exactly to sentences 6.53, 6.54, and 7. Thus, one could include 6.521–2 or 6.5n, or 6.n as frame remarks. According to Wittgenstein's explanation of the numbering system of the *Tractatus* in the sole footnote of the book, the 'ending' must be TLP 7, whereas 6.53–4 explain or clarify 6.5, which in turn elucidates the significance of TLP 6. Accordingly, the very idea of the ending/conclusion as part of the frame is unclear. Actually, whatever ending Wittgenstein had in mind in his letter, his instructions concerning the number system demand an explanation of the ending 'frame' as part of the transition from TLP 6 to 7, which is absent in the resolute reading.[12]

---

[12] Diamond (2019, 5) says that a "minor change" in her views has taken place. Now she thinks that "the image of the 'frame' of the *Tractatus* turned out to be unhelpful." She does not explain, however, why it turned out that way. It is also not clear why it is a minor change, for the 'frame' has been used as a distinctive mark of the resolute reading.

The reading also lacks an explanation for the use and status of the logical symbolism of the *Tractatus*. Diamond argues in her early work that Wittgenstein's goal is "to describe a way of writing sentences, a way of translating ordinary sentences into a completely perspicuous form" (1996: 184). This suggests that nonsense cannot be written in the symbolism when it is analyzed, which seems to imply that the symbolism is a criterion of sense. Also 'bipolarity' seems to give a criterion of sense in Diamond's reading (1996: 195–201). Thus, the symbolism seems to show that someone has failed to give meaning to signs. But even if it is just the expression of a "completely perspicuous form," and not a criterion of sense, why can it be used? Is it part of the "frame" (even if understood in its broad sense)? The later Conant argues that notations are merely "put forward as *proposals*" (Conant, 2007: 47).[13] However, even if this were correct, we would not know yet why we are able to use the notation, since there are notational devices in several parts of the book. Are these transitional remarks? In any case, the idea that Tractarian notations are "proposals" does not agree with what Wittgenstein writes about his logical symbolism. The general form of propositions, the central notational device of the book, for instance, presents the "essence of proposition" (TLP-OT: 5.471). It is "a description of . . . *any* sign-language *whatsoever*" (TLP: 4.5). Are those ironical remarks? If one allows *that* as ironical, one could equally, against Conant and Diamond, take remarks in the 'frame' as ironical and deceptive (I will deal with this in Section 1.3).

However, the idea that notations are proposals, defended by the later Conant, is part of what one could label "a radical solution" to the problematic status of a "general approach" to nonsense and the analysis of particular cases inside the resolute reading. The idea is part of the "piecemeal nonsense reading" (this is phase two of the resolute reading). According to the later Diamond and Conant, there is no general criterion of sense *at all* in the *Tractatus*: neither the logical symbolism, nor bipolarity, nor the context principle can be a general criterion of sense (Conant and Diamond, 2004: 58). Only a case-by-case study of sentences without the presupposition of a general criterion of sense could make nonsense manifest. This shift or adjustment of the reading is Goldfarb's suggestion (1997: 71). Diamond accepted it because "any propositional sign can be used in various ways" (Diamond, 2004: 203). Conant and Diamond (2004) think that according to the *Tractatus* one must take into account *how* signs and projections are *actually* meant by philosophers (case-by-case) before declaring a sentence nonsense. After trying to make sense of a nonsensical string of words, one

---

[13] Conant and Bronzo (2017: 183) claim that mastering the notation is important for "most resolute readers," but they do not say if Conant has changed his mind concerning "proposals."

might not be able to make sense of it, and then it is nonsense. Therefore, a careful examination of what a philosopher, but also Wittgenstein himself, might mean in each occasion should show that nothing is meant or projected with a nonsensical string of words. Arguably, this procedure could guarantee that the analysis of signs in sentences is theory free or even logic free.[14]

The "piecemeal nonsense reading" is puzzling. A piecemeal case-by-case procedure is part of a method that Wittgenstein only developed many years after the *Tractatus*, in a quite different context (Engelmann, 2013: 65–112). The resolute reading projects Wittgenstein's later work into the *Tractatus*.[15] One does not find hints of the effective wish or need to use such a method at the time of the *Tractatus*. Moreover, if the resolute reader (or Wittgenstein) is not able to make sense of something, it does not mean that it does not make sense. One's ability to make sense might be limited.[16] Later, when Wittgenstein indeed introduced a case-by-case approach, the point was that the procedure stops when the one speaking nonsense recognizes it as nonsense, when he, as it were, sees himself in a mirror. Nothing of the sort can be found in the *Tractatus*. Had Wittgenstein really defended a piecemeal conception of nonsense in the *Tractatus*, *if* the need for analysis existed in the case of nonsense, *his* idea of analysis would have to play a role. Analysis is a process of interpretation that ends with logically independent elementary propositions and simple names. However, such ideas never play a role in the "piecemeal" analysis of Conant and Diamond.

This point is relevant for two reasons. Wittgenstein does not appeal to any analysis, be it Hacker's combinatorial objects or Diamond's criterion-free analysis, in order to call sentences 'nonsense.' This strongly suggests that neither procedure is needed (see Sections 3.3–3.4). Second, although analysis is not used to determine the nonsensicality of strings of words, analysis is clearly fundamental, for it is used to clarify the *sense* of propositions grounded in logically independent elementary propositions (see Section 2.3). It is an idea that Wittgenstein criticized and abandoned when he returned to philosophy in 1929 (see RLF). He did so in order to deal with "statements of degree," whose

---

[14] See Kuusela (2011) for arguments against resolute readers who "throw away" the symbolism of the *Tractatus*.

[15] The projection of the late into the early Wittgenstein is also present in McGinn's idea of "assembling reminders" (2006: 33) and Moyal-Sharrock's idea that Tractarian elucidations are "grammatical rules" that determine the "bounds of sense" (2007: 182). These anachronisms are certainly unwarranted. They distort the *Tractatus* and obliterate the need for the introduction of the later ideas in Wittgenstein's philosophy. "Grammatical rule," for instance, is introduced precisely because something went wrong in the *Tractatus*. For how the later ideas are introduced, see Engelmann (2013).

[16] This reminds one of Humpty-Dumpty. See Engelmann (2018a).

analysis seemed to be incompatible with the *Tractatus*.[17] It is here that one sees why the idea of analysis of the *Tractatus* does not work without modifications. Conant and Diamond do not account for these facts.

1.3 "Understanding the Author": Not a Resolute Method of Deception

For Conant and Diamond, "understanding the author" means understanding that Wittgenstein misleads the reader with the "illusion of sense." Supposedly, Wittgenstein creates the illusion of sense with a "strategy of deception" grounded in an ironical procedure or authorial 'method.' The resolute reading seems to replace the mystical reading's appeal to influences on Wittgenstein with Conant's reinterpretation of Kierkegaard's idea of 'indirect communication' (see Section 1.1). According to him, contrary to mystical readings, Wittgenstein communicates indirectly that there is nothing to be reached 'beyond the paradox.'[18] The book works as a kind of therapy for philosophical nonsense.

For Conant, the real method of the *Tractatus* mirrors what he thinks is Kierkegaard's: paradoxical claims are introduced so that the reader can realize for herself that they say nothing and are just an expression of illusion of sense once she understands the author Wittgenstein, and not his propositions. Kierkegaard and Wittgenstein present a "mock doctrine" that appears to make sense, but is just the expression of a "strategy of deception" (Conant, 1995: 286, 293). An "incessant activity of irony" might make the reader aware of the "pseudo-doctrine" used by the author (Conant, 1993: 215–16). One must conclude that understanding Wittgenstein's irony and strategy of deception means understanding – either step by step (piecemeal view) or at the end of the book holding on to a frame (frame view) – that he presented merely a "mock doctrine" that we must abandon in order to get rid of philosophical illusion (Conant, 1995: 282–6).

An initial problem with such a view is that Conant provides no evidence to show that Wittgenstein had read a good deal of Kierkegaard at the time, that he was aware of what Conant believes was Kierkegaard's 'method,' and that he was willing to use it. Conant mentions a letter that Russell wrote to Lady Ottoline on 20 December 1919, where he says that Wittgenstein was reading "people like Kierkegaard" (Conant, 1993: 196).[19] Since this took place at least

---

[17] See Engelmann (2013), (2017), and (2018b).

[18] Details on "understanding the author" and Kierkegaard appear in Conant's work, but Diamond agrees with Conant's strategy – Diamond (1996: 18, 198; 2000: 160); Conant and Diamond (2004: 82).

[19] See Russell (2002: 334).

a year after the *Tractatus* was written, it is not sufficiently relevant, particularly because there is no reference at all to Kierkegaard in the *Tractatus* and in the *Notebooks*.

In fact, Conant could have argued that there is a relevant reference to Kierkegaard in a letter from Hermine to Wittgenstein from 20 November 1917, when the last version of the *Tractatus* was not yet completely finished. She writes: "I selected a few volumes [of Kierkegaard's works] at random because I don't know anything about him or his writings" (WFL: 75).[20] If Wittgenstein did not ask for anything specific, and his sister made a random choice, he had no specific works in mind. Thus, he was not reading Kierkegaard systematically at the end of 1917. However, the understanding of Conant's version of Kierkegaard's method depends on quite systematic reading of several works (I come back to this below). Moreover, at the end of 1917, Wittgenstein had already written more than one version of the *Tractatus* with variations in the numbering of sentences. Nothing suggests that he reinvented his method.

Fortunately, there is direct evidence that Wittgenstein was aware of Kierkegaard's "strategy of deception" *years later*, in a manuscript from 1931. However, it is precisely Wittgenstein's awareness of the strategy that shows that he did *not* employ it in the *Tractatus*. There are two quite relevant passages from 1931, where Wittgenstein refers to both, Kierkegaard's irony and his strategy of deception. In the first, Wittgenstein points out that Kierkegaard's irony "inclines the reader to become presumptuous" (PPO: 77). Thus, it has bad consequences. The second relevant passage is the following:

> Kierkegaard's writings have something teasing (*etwas Neckendes*) in them and this is, naturally, intended [...] And I know quite well that with his mastery of it Kierkegaard reduces the aesthetic to absurdity & that of course he wants to do that [...]
>
> The idea that someone employs a trick in order to get me to do something is unpleasant. It is *certain* that in order to do this (in order to employ this trick) one needs a lot of courage and [it is certain] that I *would not* have this courage – *not even remotely* [would I have the courage]. But the question is whether it would be good|correct to employ it [the trick], if I had this courage. I believe that besides courage, it would require lack of love for the neighbor. (PPO: 131; slightly modified translation; my emphasis)

For Kierkegaard, the "aesthetic" is a typical point of view in modernity. It is shallow and dodges ethical and religious commitments. He presents "the aesthetic" and its speculations by means of pseudonyms, for instance, Victor

---

[20] In Engelmann (2018a) I was not aware of this reference.

Eremita in *Either/Or*, who is the editor of letters of *A* and *B*, and Johannes Climacus in the *Concluding Unscientific Postscript to the Philosophical Crumbs*. The pseudonymous works should prepare the reader for and lead her to Kierkegaard's religious works (for instance, *For Self-Examination*). For the goal of his work as a whole is religious, as he explains in *Point of View for my Work as an Author*. In this work, he says that he begins where the reader is, i.e., in an aesthetic point of view, in order to free her from it and its illusions. As a result, the reader might accept a religious point of view, which for Kierkegaard means living a true Christian life.

Note that according to the first part of the passage above, Wittgenstein does not identify the strategy of deception with a "mock doctrine" or as anything connected with an "illusion of sense," as Conant's reading of Kierkegaard requires. Nonetheless, it is clear that Wittgenstein was aware of Kierkegaard's trick, his 'deceiving strategy' and teasing irony. Wittgenstein sees that Kierkegaard teases the aesthetic reader, presumably with irony, in order to bring "the aesthetic to absurdity" (PPO: 131). This gives some support to Conant's view, *provided* that the idea of a "mock doctrine" is abandoned, for Wittgenstein is aware of Kierkegaard's trick of deception.

However, the second part of the quote above attests that the trick was *not* used in the *Tractatus*. Wittgenstein certainly would not even *remotely*, as he writes, have the courage to employ Kierkegaard's trick of deception. Bringing the reader to the "right view" by means of deception is a trick that he simply would *never* use. If the remarks had been written before the *Tractatus*, one could still suppose a change of mind, although showing that such a change really took place would require extraordinary evidence. However, since they were written many years after (in 1931), there is no question of a change of mind. The fact that Wittgenstein was *certain* that he *would not, even remotely*, have the courage to employ Kierkegaard's strategy, excludes such a change and, thus, he certainly did not use it in the *Tractatus*.

The most troubling feature of the story about a resolute method of deception is that it ends up concealing the real method of the book, which is otherwise open to view. 'Method' as the possible method of the book appears twice: as what "the correct method in philosophy would really be" (TLP: 6.53) and as "my method" (TLP 4.1121). "*My* method" and what "the correct method" *would* be are not the same. Evidently, Wittgenstein neither says "propositions of natural science," nor waits for someone to say something metaphysical in the book, as prescribed by the would-be method in TLP 6.53. As Diamond (2000: 155) correctly pointed out, the would-be method is not the method followed in the *Tractatus*. However, contrary to the resolute reading, "my method" really and simply means "my study of sign-language" (TLP: 4.1121). This method consists in the study of such terms as 'proposition,' 'language,' and 'logic,' all made clear in a new symbolism. I will return to *Wittgenstein's* method in Sections 2 and 3 in order to explain how it is developed and applied, respectively.

Finally, the very attribution of an ironical-authorial method or procedure to the *Tractatus* by resolute readers is puzzling. When someone says something ironical, we do not take this person at his word. However, resolute readers usually accuse other readers of not taking Wittgenstein seriously, at his word. The biggest problem here is that any reader can interpret the so-called 'irony' of the *Tractatus* in a quite particular way. Metaphysical readers might claim, for instance, that TLP 6.54 is merely an ironical remark, with which Wittgenstein ironically deceives readers into thinking that his "metaphysically necessary" propositions, as Hacker calls them, are mere nonsense. Following Janik and Toulmin, one might claim that there is "Krausian irony" in TLP 6.54 suggesting that "[Tractarian] nonsense is anything but *unimportant*" (1973: 199). It is clear that if we bring irony into the game as a decisive move, rules for reading the book might vanish, for each reader might end up taking a different remark as ironical, and then any interpretation is allowed. This would be a kind of interpretational paradox.

1.4 Discontents

Although reasons vary, dissatisfaction with the metaphysical excesses of the traditional reading and the merely therapeutic approach of the resolute reading are the most common grounds for proposing a third alternative.[21] The most systematic work along these lines is McGinn's *Elucidating the Tractatus* (2006). It presents a comprehensive 'elucidatory' reading covering TLP 1 through 6, drawing on work by Rhees, Ishiguro, Winch, and McGuinness,[22] and offers a detailed alternative to both metaphysical and resolute readings. She agrees with Diamond and Conant's critique of the "traditional reading," but thinks that they do not do justice to the "positive insights" of the *Tractatus* (McGinn, 2006: 6).

Particularly insightful is the twist given to the so-called 'ontology,' a Tractarian topic that had never received such a systematic treatment from a critique of the metaphysical tradition. McGinn thinks that the status of the "opening remarks" of the *Tractatus* should "undergo a change of aspect" (2006: 137). However, this does not mean that we should see the 'ontology' destroyed

---

[21] See, for instance, Reid (1998), Biletzki (2003), Hutto (2003), Sullivan (2004), Stern (2004), White (2006), Moyal-Sharrock (2007), Cahill (2011), Lugg (2013).

[22] The book does not cover the sentences following TLP 6. The significance of those is explained in Sections 4.1–4.5.

as a "mock doctrine," as suggested by the resolute reading, but that the 'ontology' is simply not the hypothesis of a "transcendent reality" given independently of language (McGinn, 2006: 137). When we advance in the *Tractatus*, according to McGinn, we should see the 'ontology' as somehow internal to projective relations in language, in "the context of a system of representation" (2006: 17–19, 132–40). What at first looked like metaphysical remarks expressing a doctrine are really "at bottom, an articulation of the logic, that is, essence of depiction" (McGinn, 2006: 137). This articulation is presented by elucidations of ordinary language, and is not part of an ineffable theory or doctrine: Wittgenstein wants us to see what is already present and known in the ordinary use of language (McGinn, 1999: 501–3). Properly understood, sentences about ontology are "no more than a description of the logical order that is revealed by the investigation of the logic of depiction" (McGinn, 2006: 147).

Initially, McGinn (1999) argued that we should distinguish between what is and what is not 'elucidatory.' The logical symbolism, for instance, was not part of the "elucidatory core," whereas the picture conception of language was (498). It seems that she changed her mind in McGinn (2006), for there the symbolism appears as part of the elucidatory core and logic is the essence of depiction (137). McGinn sees that taking one set or other of remarks as elucidatory inherits the difficulties of the 'frame' story, for in principle all remarks of the *Tractatus* are elucidatory and nonsensical (TLP: 4.112, 6.54). Consequently, the best approach would be to consider that the book consists "entirely of elucidations," because no doctrine or theory of meaning grounds the claim that its propositions are nonsense (McGinn, 2006: 17). However, McGinn's strategy has a problem. Whether the book's "elucidatory core" is restricted to a part or includes the entire book, whether or not it is part of a doctrine, the elucidatory sentences are still nonsensical. Our apparent self-defeating paradox is not 'if the *doctrine* of the *Tractatus* is true, its sentences are nonsense,' but 'if its *sentences* are true or correct elucidations, then its sentences are nonsense.'

McGinn's account of the 'ontology' makes this difficulty manifest. She argues that "description of the logical order" implies that "the *meanings* of the primitive expressions of our language are essential to the descriptions of any world, real or imaginary" (McGinn, 2006: 154; my emphasis). Those meanings are "the unalterable form common to all worlds" (McGinn, 2006: 155). This essentialist view of objects reminds one of metaphysical readings. Her strategy, then, is to reduce it to the idea that any possible world has always the same basic *words* (McGinn, 2006: 150–1). However, it is not clear how *meanings* "must be common between an imagined and the real one," if, as she argues, "the meaning of the names exist simply insofar as the name exists" (McGinn, 2006: 151).

Meanings, it seems, cannot have both roles simultaneously. Besides, if Wittgenstein's point was simply to elucidate the system of representation in language, he could have done that without an account of objects. Against metaphysical readings, she argues that whereas the talk about things as independent of language in the *Tractatus* is incorrect, the talk about words is correct (say, syntax instead of ontology). The problem now is that talk about words is as nonsensical in Tractarian terms as talk about things.[23] Wittgenstein does not distinguish, say, syntactical and ontological remarks. The former are as nonsensical as the latter (TLP: 4.1272).

We will see in Section 2 a different explanation for the role of the 'ontology' and in Sections 2 and 3 how this role relates to the showing symbolism of the book. This will allow us to eliminate the apparent self-defeating character of the *Tractatus* (Section 3.5).

1.5 Benchmarks for a Reading and "Overlapping Consensus"

Drawing on the variety of readings seen above, we can now identify some benchmarks for the correct reading of the *Tractatus*. First, we must explain how and why the book is not "self-defeating" or "paradoxical." If nothing else, exegetical charity demands this. Second, we must explain how and to what extent the *Tractatus* could indeed end metaphysics, since Wittgenstein claimed to have solved "in essentials" the problems of philosophy. Third, we must explain how the imperative of silence presented in TLP 7 relates to TLP 6 and 6.n, which drive us to it. This then might explain the "ethical point" of the book. Fourth, 2.0n, where the so-called 'ontology' of the *Tractatus* is presented, must be elucidated in agreement with the solution of the problem of self-defeat and the solution "in essentials" of philosophical problems (TLP: preface). Fifth, we must account for Wittgenstein's changes of view in his middle period and his discovery of specific mistakes in the *Tractatus*.

---

[23] Kuusela calls himself a 'resolute reader,' but he is perhaps closer to McGinn, for he thinks that Tractarian logic must give us positive insights (2019: 37–44) and that, apparently disagreeing with Diamond and Conant, bipolarity is a criterion of sense (2019: 103). He brings Tractarian elucidations close to Carnap's syntactical principles, and argues that there is no "paradox of nonsensical theses" because "introducing logical or syntactical concepts and principles" is not yet presenting a theory, and because sentences of the *Tractatus* are "reminders" of what we already know (Kuusela, 2019: 92–3) – in this, his move is similar to McGinn (2006: 33). His comparison between Tractarian 'showing' and Carnap's 'formal mode of speech' ('syntax') is helpful and insightful, but also misleading when he claims that they are "essentially the same" (Kuusela, 2019: 103). This implies that nonsensical 'syntactical' remarks *show* something. Besides, if "speaking in the material mode" (Kuusela, 2019: 103) is *saying*, nonsensical 'ontological' remarks in the *Tractatus* say something. See Section 1.1 for why Carnap and Neurath worried about Tractarian 'elucidations.'

Except for the fifth, which is not my topic here,[24] all benchmarks are accounted for in a unitary fashion in this Element. Beginning with the so-called 'ontology' and method in Section 2, I move to the unity of the logic of language and the paradox in Section 3, and deal with the solution in essentials of the problems of philosophy and the ending of the book in Section 4. This movement presents the central argument of the *Tractatus*, which shows the nature of Wittgenstein's formal-linguistic conception of philosophy.

Instead of incorporating insights from various readings in a unifying effort or finding a middle way, I wish to offer a platform on which readers can agree and, consequently, reconsider some of their views. Thus, I aim at what Rawls (2001: 32–8) called an 'overlapping consensus,' in which the requirements above and their fulfilment should capture what one reasonably expects from a reading of the book.

2 Method, Analysis, and Ontology

2.1 Background

Frege and Russell are the fundamental influences on the *Tractatus*, and the understanding of both is required for an appreciation of its details.[25] However, as seen in Section 1, while Russell's philosophy is the natural entrance to the *Tractatus* for metaphysical readers, Frege's views ground generally non-metaphysical readings. Here, I will engage metaphysical readings at their starting point. By considering Wittgenstein's struggle with Russell, I offer a reevaluation of the so-called 'ontology' and, at the same time, of the method of the *Tractatus* – a recurrent theme in the resolute reading.

Goldfarb (2002) argued that the sophisticated reading of Frege attributed to Wittgenstein by resolute readers is not well grounded. Wittgenstein was not sufficiently aware of the details of Frege's philosophy in order to be working "within" Frege's views (Goldfarb, 2002: 186). Be that as it may, what matters most for us here is that everything in the pre-*Tractatus* writings (letters, NL,

---

[24] Chapters 1, 3, and 5 of Engelmann (2013) present three different *kinds* of critiques that Wittgenstein made of the *Tractatus*. The first dates from immediately after his return to philosophy, the second in the *Big Typescript*, and the third in *Philosophical Investigations*. On the first critique, see also Engelmann (2018b) and (2017).

[25] Wittgenstein's recognition of the influence of the writings of "my friend Bertrand Russell" as the stimulus of his thoughts is not less valuable than his recognition of Frege's "great works" (TLP: preface). "My friend" indicates a common treatment that expresses great proximity in the development of a common project. It parallels Russell's previous references to "my friend Mr. Wittgenstein" in a footnote in *Theory of Knowledge* (1913: 46), and to "vitally important discoveries, not yet published, by my friend Mr. Wittgenstein" in the preface of *Our Knowledge of the External World* (1914a: 12). Later, in the preface of *The Philosophy of Logical Atomism*, Russell mentions again "my friend and former pupil Ludwig Wittgenstein" (1918: 35).

NM, and NB) points to the fact that Wittgenstein was working "within" Russell's philosophy. In Russell's works, Wittgenstein found an early agenda, a common project, and a set of shared philosophical problems.[26] Already in December 1912, Wittgenstein told Russell that he was working on "*our* theory of symbolism" (WC: 36; my emphasis). In 1913, according to Pinsent, Wittgenstein was expected to rewrite the first eleven chapters of *Principia Mathematica* (see McGuinness, 1988: 180). After finishing the *Tractatus*, Wittgenstein told Russell he had "solved *our* problems finally" (WC: 89; my emphasis). Thus, Russell's views and their problems are fundamental throughout.

We shall see that the role of the so-called 'ontology' in the *Tractatus*, is best understood as a quite specific response to problems in Russell's philosophy around 1912–3 (Sections 2.5–2.6). Thus we first need to identify the relevant details of Russell's philosophy (Section 2.2). As we saw in Section 1.3, the real method of the *Tractatus* is simply Wittgenstein's "study of sign-language" (TLP 4.1121). We will see how this method arises out of Wittgenstein's struggle with Russell's philosophy and method, and how it is connected with the general strategy of the *Tractatus* (Section 2.3–2.4). These points will help us see how the whole argument of the *Tractatus* works, particularly because the clash between Russell's and Wittgenstein's views concerning philosophical problems gives us a key to both the general argument and the ending of the *Tractatus* (Sections 3 and 4).

2.2 Open Questions in Russell's Philosophy

In *Problems of Philosophy*, understanding or judging an atomic proposition *aRb* is a multiple relation that relates the subject and the components a, R, and b. *R* is a relation; *a* and *b* are particulars. Components of an atomic proposition are things in reality, and not intermediaries like Fregean senses or mental representations. A proposition *aRb* is true if the complex aRb exists, otherwise false. If the complex does not exist, the components of the complex do exist, although not in the judged combination (Russell, 1912: 128–9).

What grounds Russell's theory is direct acquaintance: "Every proposition which we can understand must be composed wholly of constituents with which we are acquainted" (Russell, 1912: 58). The components of atomic complexes and propositions are objects and universals (properties, relations, etc.). We can

---

[26] Landini (2007) correctly highlights the fact that Wittgenstein was Russell's "pupil," and not Frege's, and that he began serious work in philosophy because of Russell's encouragement. However, one of Landini's controversial claims is that Russell was not committed to the fundamental role of a sense-datum epistemology. This is contradicted by the fact that Wittgenstein and Russell themselves understood Russell's philosophy in this way, as we will see.

only "speak significantly" if we attach meanings (objects) to words, "and the meaning we attach to our words must be something with which we are acquainted" (Russell, 1912: 58). Thus, for Russell *understanding is* acquaintance with components of propositions and complexes. It is this theory of direct acquaintance together with the theory of descriptions that allows Russell to eliminate not only entities like Fregean senses but also mental images or 'contents,' intermediaries between words and things that are usually assumed in explanations of how words and sentences are meaningful (Russell, 1913: 41–4).

There are at least four relevant problems with Russell's theory. First, in *Problems of Philosophy* Russell sees that a new element must be introduced in his theory of judgment, namely the sense (order), for the components of the complex in asymmetrical relations like 'a before b' and 'b before a' and non-symmetrical relations like 'a loves b' and 'b loves a' are the same, but the senses are different. Therefore, it seems that more than mere acquaintance with objects is required to understand a proposition. Second, Russell's acquaintance-based analysis must explain the unity of the proposition: how a "comprehensive relation" brings constituents into relation to each other (Russell, 1913: 112). Constituents plus 'sense' are not enough to explain unity. Since 'sense' (order) itself must be already part of true complexes, it cannot be what unites complexes *in thought* (Russell, 1913: 116). Thus, a certain relational form must unify and organize the complex in a judgment. Note that the relational form must guarantee that "judgments" such as the nonsensical "love Cassio Desdemona" never take place. According to Wittgenstein in a letter to Russell from January 1913, type theory is the guarantee: "I want a theory of types to tell me that 'Mortality is Socrates' is nonsensical" (WC: 38).[27] Third, Russell had no theory of judgments for molecular propositions while he was in contact with Wittgenstein between 1911 and 1914, but any extension of his theory for atomic propositions would have implied the existence of logical objects/constants (Russell, 1913: 99, 130). Such a view would have made it very difficult to grasp the nature of inference, since presumably various complexes and kinds of objects are present in the relation between premises and conclusion.

The fourth problem can be formulated as "How does analysis end?" The logical representation of a sentence like "The present king of France is bald" seems to be *Fa*. One is inclined to think that its constituents are the name 'the

---

[27] Russell's theory of types was created in order to avoid a series of paradoxes, including the following: "the class of all classes that are not members of themselves is (or is not) a member of itself" (if it is, then it is not; if it is not, then it is). The string of words "the class ... " is nonsense, and not simply false, for the quantification over all classes violates distinctions of types of classes (classes of individuals, classes of classes of individuals, etc.).

present king of France' (*a*) and the universal or propositional function 'x is bald' (*Fx*). The trouble is that since the mentioned king does not exist, it seems that we cannot say that the negation of the sentence is true, even though the sentence seems to be false. It looks like a violation of the law of the excluded middle (Fa ∨ ~Fa). Thus, we would be inclined to say that "The present king of France is bald" is nonsense, because the expression 'the present king of France' does not refer to anything. As is well known, according to Russell, phrases like 'the present king of France' have meaning only in the context of a sentence whose real logical form is *(∃x) (Kx ∧ (y) (Ky → x=y) ∧ Bx)*, where Kx is the function 'x is king of France' and Bx is 'x is bald.' This contextual definition shows that the sentence does not violate the law of the excluded middle.

According to Russell, analysis introduces an existential quantifier and bound variables ('apparent variables') in the case of ordinary names as well. A named object might not exist, and one might ask, for instance, whether Moses existed. In this case, one might mean '*the* leader of the Israelites when they came out of Egypt.' Thus, what we mean by an ordinary proper name is expressed with definite descriptions, for they determine the thing we have in mind, and they apply even when the object named does not exist. Properly understood, ordinary names hide definite descriptions, and therefore introduce quantifiers with bound variables when translated into the logical symbolism (Russell, 1905: 54). Those variables must vary over something named by *real* proper names, logically speaking. For without real proper names, either the problem of the excluded middle reappears or analysis never ends.

In *Principia Mathematica*, Russell argued that the analysis of propositions must come to an end. Ultimately, the theory of acquaintance, and its finite apprehension, requires the end of analysis. Russell argues that "no proposition which we can apprehend can contain more than a finite number of apparent variables, on the ground that whatever we can apprehend must be of finite complexity" (Russell and Whitehead, 1910: 50). This means that the 'source' of complex propositions is a function *fx* of "finite complexity," whose apprehension is exemplified in atomic propositions *fa, fb, fc*, etc. This raises the question: what are the atomic propositions and the real simple names?

Russell's tentative answer is epistemological. Since names cannot fail to name when they occur in atomic propositions, one must find names that name no matter what. Since one can be absolutely certain of the existence of 'objects of perception' (sense-data) given by acquaintance as sensations, they are 'a something' *whatever* is the case. They exist and can be named even if we hallucinate or dream: "when we dream or see a ghost, we certainly do have the sensations we think we have" (Russell, 1912: 19). Thus, if we judge by referring to perceptions (personal experience) like in "This is red" or "the redness of this," our judgment "must be true" (Russell and Whitehead, 1910: 43). Thus, 'this' in atomic propositions like 'This is red' is a real logical name (Russell, 1913: 39).

Therefore, the ultimate ground for logic and epistemology is the experience of acquaintance with particulars and universals. Supposedly, acquaintance explains understanding and guarantees the certainty of what is given. Because of the need for a similar account of molecular propositions, acquaintance must also be extended to logical objects such as negation, disjunction, all, some, etc. (Russell, 1913: 98). Thus, "logical experience" grounds logic: "there certainly is such a thing as *'logical experience'*, by which I mean that kind of immediate knowledge, other than judgment, which is what enables us to understand logical terms" (Russell, 1913: 97; my emphasis).[28]

Before we move to Wittgenstein's own views, some aspects of Russell's scientific method in philosophy must be introduced, for the contrast of methods will give us important clues here and in Sections 3.1 and 4.1–4.5. For Russell, philosophy's task is the understanding of "the general aspects of the world and the logical analysis of familiar but complex things" (Russell, 1914a: 28). The philosopher with a scientific spirit applies doubt to common-sense beliefs and discovers the indubitable "hard data" of philosophy: logic and those sense-data given in acquaintance (Russell, 1914a: 77–8). The hard data guide an inventory of logical forms and the expression of general formal truths. These truths are "supremely general propositions, which assert the truth of all propositions of certain form" (Russell, 1914a: 67). In this view, "the discovery of the logical form of the facts ... is the hardest part of the work" (Russell, 1914b: 86–7). Philosophical propositions "must be general" and "must be a priori," neither proved nor disproved by experience, and as the "science of the possible," philosophy becomes "indistinguishable from logic" (Russell, 1914b: 86).

2.3 Wittgenstein's Reformation

During 1912, Wittgenstein was involved in developing Russell's theory of judgment for molecular propositions (WC: 30, 32, 34). Very early, however, he was certain that the right explanation of apparent variables was that "there are NO logical constants" (WC: 30). Soon after, he comes to think that there is no way to deal with molecular propositions unless atomic ones are clearly understood: "I believe that our problems can be traced down to the *atomic* propositions" (WC: 35). At the beginning of 1913, Wittgenstein arrives at the first idea that put him at odds with Russell's philosophy: "every theory of types must be

---

[28] For detailed accounts of problems in Russell's philosophy that are relevant for understanding the *Tractatus*, see Hylton (1992), Ricketts (1996), Kremer (1997), and Potter (2011).

rendered superfluous by a proper theory of the symbolism" so that "whatever can be symbolized by a simple proper name must belong to one type" (WC: 38).

Wittgenstein wanted a theory of atomic propositions that did not rely on type theory. In the new theory, "Qualities, Relations (like love), etc., are all copulae" (WC: 38). What he meant at that time was that complexes like "Socrates is human" would be a composition of 'Socrates' and 'something is human' ($\exists x\ Hx$), both components presumed simple. In the old view from 1912, type theory should guarantee that one cannot judge a nonsense like "Humanity is Socrates" (WC: 38). The new theory should dispense with type theory because the symbols themselves, being of different kinds, should make clear that a wrong substitution is not possible, since only a name can take the place of the objectual variable.[29]

Wittgenstein abandoned type theory because it did not seem plausible anymore. He makes this point in 1913:

> We can never distinguish one logical type from another by attributing a property to members of the one which we deny to members of the other. (NL: 98)

If the theory of types is useful, it must tell us that the type function (x is human) or the universal 'humanity' cannot be taken as the subject in an occurrence with the type particular (Socrates) because they are of different types. However, this very expression is nonsensical according to the theory of types itself, since presumably one can only talk meaningfully if one respects types, which is not the case in the sentence above. In *Principia Mathematica,* this problem is acute when Russell explains "being of the same type" (Russell and Whitehead, 1910: 133). As Hylton (2005: 67) argued, if "x is of the same type as a" is doing any work, i.e., if this function is a criterion for distinguishing types, it expresses a propositional function that is true or false of objects of different types. Otherwise, types cannot be successfully distinguished. Thus, "attributing a property," as Wittgenstein put it, by means of a propositional function "a is of the same type as x" should be significant in the case of entities b and c whatever they are. Suppose b is an individual and c is not. In this case, however, the propositional function "a is of the same type as x" violates type restrictions, for the theory prohibits the talk about things of different types in

---

[29] In his groundbreaking work about *Notes on Logic*, Potter (2011) identifies a "symbolic turn" in Wittgenstein's first attempts to solve his and Russell's difficulties concerning atomic propositions, and shows in well-articulated details many of its consequences. In disagreement with Potter (2011: 116, 241), I do not see the "symbolic turn" as expressed by an inference or a deduction from simples in language to simples in the world. These points are elucidated in the following sections.

one sentence. Thus, the function must be nonsense (non-significant). Thus, type theory cannot really "distinguish one logical type from another" (NL: 98).

As we saw above, Wittgenstein's first move was to replace the supposition of types with the idea that any judgment presupposes a *simple* form like *(∃R, x, y) xRy*. Expressed in words, that form appears as "something has some relation to something." Russell adopted Wittgenstein's view in his *Theory of Knowledge*: "the form of all subject-predicate complexes will be *the fact* 'something has some predicate'; the form of all dual complexes will be 'something has some relation to something' " (Russell, 1913: 114; my emphasis).

However, contrary to what their shared theory of judgment presupposed, '((∃ R, x, y) xRy)' does not look like a name of a simple at all. Wittgensten soon realized that there is a mistake in such a supposition:

> It is easy to suppose that only such symbols are complex as contain names of objects, and that accordingly "(∃x, Φ) .Φx" and "(∃x, y) . xRy" must be simple. It is then natural to call the first of these the name of a form, the second the name of a relation. But in that case what is the meaning of (e.g.) "~ (∃x,y) xRy"? Can we put "not" before a name? (NL: 97)

The trouble is that expressions that were taken to refer to simple relations or forms can be negated. However, if they can be negated, they cannot be names of simples, since the negation of names is obvious nonsense (pace Frege). The idea of a simple form obliterated the distinction between name and sentence. Now, if something such as "(∃x,Φ).Φx" and "(∃x,y).xRy" can in principle be negated, then it seems that it can also be false. This implies that unless one assumes empirical propositions to be *true* of the world, a fact, the theory allows that one judges a nonsense in case the proposition is false. As Russell put it, "the form of all subject-predicate complexes will be the *fact* 'something has some predicate' " (Russell, 1913: 114).

2.4 The A Priori and the Method of the *Tractatus*

Wittgenstein's assessment that his (and Russell's) view about a "simple form" was wrong led him to a fundamental insight, which might then at least partially explain the role of the 'ontology' of the *Tractatus*. If the truth of '(∃x, Φ) Φx' is presupposed in order to give sense to a proposition, the sense of a proposition depends on the truth of another proposition:

> I thought that the possibility of truth of the proposition Φa was tied up with the fact (∃x, Φ) Φx. But it is impossible to see why Φa should only be possible if there is another proposition of the same form. Φa surely does not need any precedent. (For suppose that there existed only the two elementary

propositions "Φa" and "Ψa" and that "Φa" were false. Why should this proposition only make sense if "Ψa" is true?). (NB: 17)[30]

Wittgenstein's argument is based on the supposition that only two elementary propositions exist (in what follows we will see why this is relevant). In this case, either a different elementary proposition (Ψa) is true and guarantees that, although false, Φa makes sense, or Φa is meaningfully false, if a is a simple name, no matter what is true. The first option, Ψa being true, would guarantee the sense of Φa because Ψa implies that $(\exists x, \Phi) \Phi x$, i.e., the truth of Ψa implies that there is an object x named by a, and that there is a predicate Φ so that that form exists.[31] However, this is absurd, for in this case the sense of Φa depends on the truth of Ψa. Logic, which expresses all conditions of sense, would depend on truth, on how the world is, and would not be completely *a priori*. Thus, Φa must make sense, even if false, independently of the truth of any other proposition. In this case, contra Russell, possible forms can never be derived from the form of facts.

This means, however, that the laws of logic linked to analysis are completely a priori, and therefore independent of *actual* analysis, only if names name something independently of the truth of any proposition. This is particularly clear in $\Phi a \vee \sim \Phi a$. Logic presupposes that names at the end of analysis must name something, for otherwise an elementary proposition like Φa could be nonsensical. That Φa is an elementary proposition means that either a is Φ or it is not, but in both cases a names something, independently of the truth of any proposition that implies the existence of a form.

The new insight has at least two consequences: a specific one and a general one. The specific one is that the analysis of any proposition cannot imply that the sense of an elementary proposition depends on the truth of an elementary proposition in order to guarantee the existence of a form, expressed by means of a completely general proposition.[32] This then makes clear that analysis can

---

[30] One might wonder how the *Notebooks* can be used in the interpretation of the *Tractatus*, since, arguably, views there are not always consistent. I think that "logic must take care of itself" (NB: 1) should always guide our reading, and incompatible views should be seen as hypothetical thinking concerning a possible application of logic (see Section 2.6 for an example). Moreover, one must keep in mind that Wittgenstein sometimes states that his thoughts are not clear (see NB: 78, 79). Finally, interpretational charity should stop one from ascribing to Wittgenstein views that one believes are simply wrong (metaphysical readers violate this idea).

[31] I think that this is what grounds Wittgenstein's idea that Russell's theory of judgment allows one to judge a nonsense, whereas the right theory should guarantee that this is not possible, as Wittgenstein puts it, *without the use of any other premise* (WC: 40). The "other premise" would be either the statement that there is a fact that guarantees sense (for instance, that there is a relation between x and y) or the theory of types. Both premises violate logic's autonomy.

[32] This is why Wittgenstein reevaluates the nature of completely general propositions (see NB: 11–22).

only end when it makes no sense to ask whether the simple names really name existing objects; otherwise, sense is not determinate and the *a priori* character of logic is in question. Thus, it is the a priori status of logic that is assumed in the so-called 'argument for substance' in the *Tractatus* (TLP: 2.021n). The point is first expressed as if the 'things' were what we are talking about: "If the world had no substance, then whether a proposition had sense would depend on whether another proposition was true" (TLP: 2.0211). The idea of the argument is then presented for the case of signs: "The requirement that simple signs be possible is the requirement that sense be determinate" (TLP: 3.23). Ultimately, what Wittgenstein is trying to avoid is that a priori logic "needs a precedent," a true proposition of any sort, which is absurd (see quotation above). In Sections 3.1–3, I discuss the talk about things and signs.

The general consequence of the new insight is the Tractarian view that logic cannot depend on any precedent: on a theory of types, or on how things are, or on *any* experience whatsoever, such as Russell's theory of acquaintance. The old view was absurd precisely because it implied that logic needs a precedent, i.e., a truth more fundamental than logic itself. If logic depended on truth it seems that logic would become contingent. This is absurd, for it jeopardizes logical necessity. Therefore, the task of the philosopher is to show that logic is in place *whatever* facts are the case, that it is completely independent from how any possible world is constituted. After all, any world is possible as long as it is a logical one. In general terms, thus, *any* precedent must disappear, for "logic must take care of itself" (TLP: 5.473; NB: 1).

Consequently, the Russellian project of finding the forms of facts must be abandoned:

> Then can we ask ourselves: Does the subject-predicate form exist? Does the relational form exist? Do any of the forms exist at all that Russell and I were always talking about? (Russell would say: "Yes! That's self-evident. " Ha!)
>
> Then: if *everything* that needs to be shewn is shewn by the existence of subject-predicate SENTENCES, etc., the task of philosophy is different from what I originally supposed. **But if** that is not how it is, then what is lacking would have to be shewn by means of some **kind of experience**, and that **I regard as out of the question**. (NB: 2–3; my emphasis is in bold letters)

Sentences, and not complexes or facts, give us all we need in logic. No experience at all can be relevant to logic. Thus, all philosophical theories which ground philosophy or logic must also disappear. This by itself gives us a new method:

All theories that say: "This is how it must be, otherwise we could not philosophize" or "otherwise we surely could not live," etc., etc., must of course disappear.

My method is not to sunder the hard from the soft, but to see the hardness of the soft. (NB: 44)

For Russell, the "hard" is logical truth and facts concerning sense-data, which are indubitable facts, while the "soft" is what is doubtful (Russell, 1914a: 77–8). In a process of "scientific" doubt, Russell sunders "the hard from the soft" *facts*. For Wittgenstein, no facts whatsoever are part of the hardness of the soft, which has nothing to do with any experience. Philosophy's task is merely *to see* the hardness of the soft. Hardness is seen in ordinary language, and the task is simply to recognize hardness in "*how* language takes care of itself" (NB: 43; Wittgenstein's emphasis). This task is fundamentally the following:

My *whole* task consists in explaining the nature of the sentence [*Satz*].
That is to say, in giving the nature of all facts, whose picture the sentence *is*. (NB: 39; modified translation)[33]

However, it will turn out that the whole task, the "explanation" of the nature of the sentence (proposition), is not really an explanation in an ordinary sense. It is simply the formal presentation of the "nature of the sentence," which means that the task consists in clearly expressing features of language that show how it works essentially in contrast to its accidental features (the soft) (NB: 44; TLP: 3.34n). This fundamental point is further elucidated in Sections 3.1–3.3 and 4.1–4.2, where I show how it connects with the very structure of the *Tractatus*.

2.5 Wittgenstein's Definite Descriptions and 'Ontology'

As seen above, Russell's contextual definition of descriptions guarantees that the law of the excluded middle is in place in language as long as we commit ourselves to analysis. From Wittgenstein's point of view, however, it guarantees that the logic of ordinary language is not disrupted by a *misleading* analysis.

---

[33] According to German dictionaries (for instance, the *Duden Deutsches Universal-wörterbuch*), *Satz* colloquially means a linguistic unit consisting of words (a written or spoken sentence). According to German-English dictionaries (for instance, the *Cambridge Dictionary*), *Satz* colloquially means sentence (in other languages the same is the case). Thus, 'sentence' is the natural and neutral translation of *Satz,* and other options ask for justification. Probably because Wittgenstein's major goal is the elucidation of declarative sentences, 'proposition' has become the standard translation of *Satz*. This *might* be misleading, for someone might erroneously think that a proposition is not simply a statement, but an abstract or mental entity. In spite of this, I use 'proposition' in many cases due to editorial reasons (there are too many occurrences of *Satz* in the *Tractatus*). However, in order to keep in mind that 'proposition' is a translation of *Satz,* a linguistic unit consisting of words (a written or spoken sentence in a language in use), I use 'sentence' and the German *Satz* sometimes.

Without Russell's definition, we might consider a sentence like "The present king of France is bald" to be nonsensical, although it makes perfect sense in ordinary language. It is simply false (PI: §39). "The present king of France is bald," in spite of appearances, is in perfect logical order, for Russell shows that "a proposition that mentions a complex will not be nonsensical, if the complex does not exist, but simply false" (TLP: 3.24). Thus, Russell's contextual understanding of descriptions helps us to see that "in fact, all the propositions of our everyday language, just as they stand, are in perfect logical order" (TLP: 5.5563). Therefore, it is crucial for the philosophical task of understanding "*how* language takes care of itself" (NB: 43).

The contextual view of descriptions also indicates, formally, contra Russell, that *understanding* is a notion that is logically relevant to the extent that we specify truth conditions in *sentences*. In Russell's example, the expression of what is meant by the original sentence is, in fact, merely the presentation of truth conditions: (1) there is at least one king of France, (2) there is not more than one king of France, (3) and he is bald. Wittgenstein extracts from Russell's definition that expressing logically what one understands *is* expressing the truth conditions of a sentence. One understands a proposition when one knows what is the case if it is true and what is the case if it is not true (TLP: 4.024). If Russell's contextual definition expresses the way analysis works, it also shows that *logical* analysis ends with sentences. If something else is added (say, acquaintance), it is not logical analysis anymore. Russell's epistemological analysis is dispensable (TLP: 4.1121).

Thus, the meaning of simple names is not given in isolation by means of acquaintance, but only in the context of something with sense, i.e., a proposition: "Only propositions have sense; only in the nexus of a proposition does a name have meaning" (TLP: 3.3). Russell's own analysis already points to the significance of the contextual use of words. Phrases containing 'the' "have a meaning in use, but not in isolation," i.e., "the propositions in whose symbolic expression it occurs" (Russell and Whitehead, 1910: 67). Note, however, that since ordinary names are analyzed in terms of definite descriptions, for Russell the context principle already applies to ordinary names (see Section 2.2). The exception that Russell needed was the case of logical (simple) names, whose meaning is given by acquaintance, in isolation (Russell, 1913: 95). On Wittgenstein's view, contextual understanding must include simple names, as well as ordinary ones. If meanings of simple names were given in isolation and in sentences, as in Russell's theory of acquaintance, contextual meaning and isolated meaning could conflict. In fact, it is this possible conflict that created Russell's problem with sense and form, for the way names appeared in isolation could collide with their appearance in the unity of propositions. The problem was that if they had meaning by acquaintance, they could be part of a nonsensical proposition. Therefore, given the logical priority of the context, "it is impossible for words to appear in two different roles: by themselves and in propositions" (TLP: 2.0122). If understanding, contra Russell, is not a matter of being acquainted with objects named, there is no problem: "When we say A judges that etc., then we have to mention a whole proposition which A judges. It will not do either to mention only its constituents, or its constituents and form, but not in the proper order" (NL: 94). With the whole proposition, there is understanding and judgment only if the proposition and its negation are explained in terms of truth conditions. Constituents without propositions are irrelevant for logic (see Section 3.3).

Wittgenstein certainly accepts that Russell's understanding of descriptions commits one to atomic propositions and simple names. However, the signs of an analyzed sentence are not what Russell thought (WC: 59). First, contrary to Russell's epistemological project, there is a purely logical criterion for atomic (elementary) propositions: logical independence (NB: 90–1; TLP: 4.211, 5.134, 6.3751).[34] The simple name is the name appearing in logically independent atomic sentences (TLP: 3.202). Therefore, the criterion for simple names is contextual as well. Second, Wittgenstein eliminates a fundamental sign in Russell's contextual definition of descriptions, namely identity (TLP: 5.531–5.5321). I discuss notational aspects of the elimination of identity in Section 3.3. Here, let us just see how the issue connects with 'ontology.'

For Russell, identity was a defined sign. His principle of the indiscernibility of the identical and the identity of the indiscernible is grounded in the definition: "$x = y =: (\Phi): \Phi!x .\rightarrow. \Phi!y$ Def." Since it states that the identity of x and y means that all properties of x are properties of y, in order for this definition to work Russell needed to use the 'axiom of reducibility,' for otherwise it would violate type restrictions (Russell and Whitehead, 1910: 168–9). The axiom of reducibility $[(\exists\Psi) (x) (\Phi x \leftrightarrow \Psi!x)]$ states that properties involving totalities (for instance, 'x has all the properties of a great general') are reducible, i.e., are formally equivalent, to a property that is predicative, i.e., a property that does not involve totalities (for instance, 'x is a general'). It is clear that such an axiom is not a logical law according to the *Tractatus*, for it is not a tautology. Now, one might think that this prompts Wittgenstein to abandon identity. Moreover, one might also think that identity is to be eliminated simply because it is incompatible with the logical independence of elementary propositions. However, those are not Wittgenstein's reasons. Identity and the axiom of reducibility are problematic in themselves. Both violate the a priori character of logic, the

---

[34] For an account of logical independence, see Anscombe (1959) and Ricketts (2014).

dispensability of a "precedent." The real trouble with the axiom of reducibility is that "it is possible to imagine a world in which the axiom of reducibility is not valid" (TLP 6.1233).[35] Obviously, Russell's axiom of infinity, which asserted the existence of an infinite number of individuals, has the same problem.

Thus, Wittgenstein is really upholding the a priori character of logic when he uses his symbolism to show that logic is tautological and, therefore, eliminates the suspicious 'axioms' that might not agree with all imaginable worlds. In contrast, Russell was not observing his own rule according to which "mathematics takes us [. . .] into the region of absolute necessity, to which not only the actual world, but every possible world, must conform" (Russell, 1910: 82).

In fact, Russell's philosophy of mathematics and logic is permeated by a tension between what he wants (absolute necessity) and what he can get (a pragmatic justification of non-necessary laws). The axiom of reducibility, for instance, is justified "inductively," i.e., by its use in the derivation of fundamental propositions in class theory and the principle of identity (Russell and Whitehead, 1910: 58–60). Wittgenstein's major insights described in this section point to a way to solve this tension by means of the elucidation of the absolute a priori necessity that dispenses with any need for the justification of logical laws (see Sections 3.1–3.3 and 4.1–4.4).[36] The *Tractatus* draws out the consequences of this insight.

As in the case of the axioms of reducibility and infinity, the problem with Russell's theory of identity in logic is the assumption of something contingent. Wittgenstein expresses the point in the following way:

> Russell's definition of '=' is inadequate because according to it we cannot say that two objects have all their properties in common. (Even if this proposition is never correct, it still has sense). (TLP: 5.5302)

Of course, in *our* world, which in any case we do not know a priori, we have not found yet a case of two things having all properties in common. Perhaps, we should rather say that "to say of *two* things that they are identical is nonsense" (TLP: 5.5303), for we usually simply exclude such a possibility. However, when we do not accept that there could be *two* identical things, we do not do so grounded in logic, according to Wittgenstein. Logically, one can imagine, for instance, a world with three objects a, b, and c, and properties Φ and Ψ. Suppose that a, b, and c are names of three objects and that 'Φa,' 'Φb,' and 'Ψc' are the

---

[35] Wittgenstein argues in the following way: "imagine we lived in a world in which nothing existed except ℵ *things* and, over and above them, ONLY a *single* relation holding between infinitely many of the things and in such a way that it did not hold between each thing and further never held between a finite number of things" (WC: 58). In such a world, there is no type 'reduction,' since there is a single relation among infinite things, and the axiom does not apply.

[36] A parallel, but different, tension operates in Frege's work. However, I cannot deal with it here.

only true propositions in a language/world. It is not impossible and it makes sense to say that things a and b have all properties in common. In fact, it is true in such a world. Therefore, Russell's theory of identity depends on contingencies, as in the case of the axioms of reducibility and infinity. Since Russell's law of identity depends on what is contingent, it is not a logical law. Russell's theory of identity is indeed a theory, a hypothesis, and as such, it can be false. Logic, however, does not depend on what can be false and what can be true (TLP: 6.1222).

The point about identity is particularly relevant because metaphysical interpreters maintain that according to the *Tractatus* all possible worlds must have the same objects (see Section 1.1). However, the argument about form discussed in Section 2.3 and the argument above show that such a view is wrong, since nothing logically *a priori* prevents us from imagining worlds with only two, three, or four objects. Indeed, the varying number of objects in possible worlds grounds Wittgenstein's critique of *all* strange "laws of logic," which are actually not logical laws at all. This is a serious shortcoming. However, metaphysical readings are also at odds with other features of the 'ontology' of the *Tractatus*. We need to go into the motivations of such readings.

2.6 The Role of 'Ontology'

What leads many readers to think that Tractarian objects are the ultimate set of objects in all possible worlds is TLP 2.02n, particularly the following sentences:

> It is obvious that an imagined world, however different it may be from the real one, must have *something* – a form – in common with it. (TLP: 2.022)
> Objects are just what constitute this unalterable [*feste*] form. (TLP: 2.023)

Note that Wittgenstein does *not* say that any world has or must have the same objects. Actually, he only says that any world has objects. The unalterable fixed *form* – and not forms in the plural – are objects. What is not subject to change, the substance, is not a specific set of objects, but the existence of objects. As seen above, logic is given *a priori* – it does not matter how *many* objects there are in any possible world. Thus, the *something* in common is the *form* object, that thing which is expressed by the simple form *x*, the object prototype. This one should see in the use of the variable *x*, the meaning of *x*, the simple prototype:

> Our simple IS: the simplest that we know. – The simplest which our analysis can attain – it need appear only as a prototype, as a variable in our propositions – *that* is the simple that we mean and look for. (NB: 47; my translation)

The simple need appear only as a variable. This is why Wittgenstein explains 2.023 by saying that the substance of the world "*can* only determine a form, and not any material properties" (TLP 2.0231). Of course, the form is 'object.' The "unalterable form" is not "the same objects in all possible worlds," but that "there are objects," whichever the number of objects in an imagined world. This boils down to "there are facts" (TLP: 2.0122). This is a *what*, and not a *how*, as Wittgenstein puts it (TLP: 5.552). Years later, Wittgenstein makes the point explicitly: "Logic depends on this: that something exists (in the sense that there is something), that there are facts" (WVC: 77). The connection of logic and world is that we are saying something *about something* no matter what is the case.

The simple is the prototype, the variable x, which appears in propositions. Thus, we should recognize as nonsensical the claims about the simple objects:

> It keeps on looking as if the question "Are there simple things?" made sense. And surely this question must be nonsense!
>
> It would be vain to try and express the pseudo-sentence "Are there simple things?" in *symbolic notation* [*Begriffsschrift*]. (NB: 45; my emphasis)

In the *Tractatus,* we are meant to overcome the nonsense about a simple thing, which is a *formal* concept, when we understand that the proper formal concept to be used is the *something* expressed in symbolic notation by means of the objectual form x (TLP: 4.1272). The very symbolism eliminates the non-sense about simples, since it is shown in the very use of the variable x that the form expresses something (I return to this in Sections 3.1–3).

Another possible confusion behind the metaphysical reading lies in Wittgenstein's talk about "forms of objects" (TLP: 2.0251). Readers who are inclined to think that the objects are the same in all possible worlds *and* that objects show which of their combinations are impossible seem to find support in a passage where Wittgenstein says that color, time, and space are forms of objects (TLP: 2.0131; quoted below). Then it seems natural to think that objects of different forms can clash.

However, one must notice again that all that is common to all possible worlds is just the form 'object,' the meaning of the variable x. That is known a priori and is shown symbolically in the variable x. Moreover, the idea of clashing forms is at odds with "objects are colorless" (TLP 2.0232). When Wittgenstein talks about color as a form of objects, he is *not* claiming that it is a *logical* form of objects. In fact, from the logical point of view of the *Tractatus*, that there is color and that we experience colors are simply empirical facts. Color, and any other specific form, is not a precedent that we need in order to understand logic. Not all worlds we can imagine have colors, and color is not a determining property of the form object. Note that the existence of colors is a fact that is even less abstract than the number of existing objects in a given world, a central issue in the elimination of identity and the axiom of reducibility. If the a priori character of logic does not allow the law of identity and the axiom of reducibility on the grounds that we can imagine a world in which they are not valid, then we should be able to imagine a world without forms like 'color.'

The interpretation presented here might also explain one of the most puzzling remarks of the *Tractatus*. Note that 2.0131, where forms are discussed, follows a sentence where Wittgenstein says that each thing is in a space of possible states of affairs, but that one "can imagine empty" this space (TLP: 2.013). Of course, we cannot imagine *logical* space empty (TLP: 5.552–5.5521). Thus, the immediate point of TLP 2.0131 is to make clear, according to the number system of the *Tractatus*, that the empty spaces are the spaces of contingent forms of objects:

> A spatial object must be situated in infinite space. (A spatial point is an argument-place.)
> A speck in the visual field, though it need not be red, must have some color: it is, so to speak, surrounded by color-space. Notes must have *some* pitch, objects of the sense of touch *some* degree of hardness, and so on. (TLP: 2.0131)

These spaces themselves are logically contingent, for they might not exist. Therefore, we can imagine them "empty," without any objects (TLP: 2.013). Again, logic has no precedent, and no experience is fundamental in logic (TLP: 5.552).

There are, indeed, logical relations ('must') expressed in the various spaces of the senses, as in the visual field (color) or the auditory space. That is, things are in spaces. However, the so-called 'ontology,' especially in TLP 2.013 and 2.0131, must be seen in the perspective of the *Tractatus* as a whole. The point about 'must' is that color is not the content of an object, because the attribution of color has formal restrictions. Since color relations are formal, there must be a hidden *formal* contradiction expressible in truth tables in the sentence that attributes two colors to an object. There is no "content contradiction" according to the *Tractatus* (TLP: 6.3751). After all, there is *only* logical necessity (TLP: 6.37). This means that the form color hides fundamental logical forms that one might find out in analysis, in the application of logic to the *actual* world. It is precisely for this reason that Wittgenstein explicitly says that propositions concerning color are *not* elementary (TLP: 6.3751). Therefore, forms like 'color' might simply vanish once concepts are analyzed, if logic, of course, agrees with its application.[37] Again: "objects are colorless" (TLP: 2.0232).

---

[37] Years after the *Tractatus*, of course, Wittgenstein found out that it does not. See Engelmann (2013) and (2017).

So why does Wittgenstein speak of sensorial spaces as forms at all? There are two reasons. First, although *a priori* logic deals with any language and, thus, any imagined world, he needs to indicate that logic is applied to the actual world (TLP: 5.557). Second, he wants to introduce the reader to logical form intuitively by means of increasing abstraction in TLP 2.1n. The point is that some pictures/models (*Bilder*) have the form of space, some the form of color, etc., but *all* are logical models that have implicit *logical* form (TLP: 2.18n-9). After all, logical form is the fundamental form, and not color, etc. Essence is expressed in logical form, and not in contingently existing forms (TLP: 5.4711).

Wittgenstein also says that the only distinction between objects of the same logical form, apart from external properties, is that "they are different" (TLP: 2.0233). If Wittgenstein is not thinking about combinatorial forms here, what does he mean? First, we should keep in mind that the identity of what is indiscernible is not a logical axiom. Thus, since the law of identity is not true a priori, and there is no theory of immediate acquaintance, if a definite description does not distinguish an object, it is a priori possible that "there are several things that have the whole set of their properties in common" (TLP: 2.02331). The identification of a single object by means of a property is a contingent matter. Of course, this is simply an expression of the non-contingency of logic grounded in the critique of Russell's theory of identity. It reflects Wittgenstein's symbolism (Section 3.3). Second, the mystery of objects of the "same form" in TLP 2.0233 dissolves, if we consider what we really know a priori "about all the possible forms of elementary propositions" as suggested in TLP 5.55. We do not know a priori if we will need, after analysis is finished, a "27-termed relation in order to signify something" (TLP: 5.5541). We are a priori "unable to give the number of names with different meanings" (TLP: 5.55). That there are "no pre-eminent numbers in logic" is a fundamental point in the *Tractatus* (TLP: 4.128, 5.453, 5.553). To give any *specific* form *a priori* would be a mistake (TLP: 5.554). This would be analogous to Russell's mistake of supposing that an "experience," which is always a contingent fact, is needed to understand logic (TLP: 5.553). Given these a priori restrictions, objects having "the same form" can only mean that in the form $\varPhi xy$, x and y share the same dual form, and that in $\varPhi xyz$, x, y, and z share the same triadic form, etc. It is because x and y in $\varPhi xy$ share the same form that the truth of a proposition with that form, and not its sense, will be determined by the order in which different variables related to different names will occur. Apart from that, only external properties distinguish them (color, for instance).

Note that, in principle, analysis could show that all relations are 4-termed, all sharing the same form. In such a case, Wittgenstein points out later, "we couldn't talk of 2-termed" in "atomic logic" (LC: 252). He explains the point further:

Suppose you talk of "molecular logic" & "atomic logic."

Now I said: "molecular logic" forms a system, independent of experience, which I can just write down. But "atomic logic" may *shew* you *that "2-term relation" has a meaning, but "4-term" none* [. . .] *I was right in thinking there can't be hypotheses in logic.* (LC: 252–3; my emphasis)

The *Tractatus* does not assume hypotheses concerning specific forms. It assumes a possible "enumeration of entities in the world" and "therefore" an enumeration of "all possible atomic propositions" (LC: 255). It is this enumeration at the end of analysis that reveals the particular forms of atomic propositions (TLP 5.55n), and not forms somehow intrinsic to 'kinds' of objects, supposedly given as determinants of language. Kinds would express external properties, which are not essential to logic.

In Tractarian terms, combinatorial kinds jeopardize logic. Suppose that there were kinds of objects that *cannot* be combined. If the 'cannot' means logical necessity, then kinds are irrelevant, for necessity is expressed only in purely formal terms: tautologies and contradictions not restricted to kinds. If the 'cannot' means a different sort of necessity, then the idea contradicts the view that there is only "*logical* necessity" (TLP: 6.37). Moreover, what kind of necessity would that be? Whatever the kind, if not tautological, logic would depend on particularities of the world (spatiality, color, sounds, etc.).

Thus, what distinguishes x and y in Φxy is indeed simply the fact "that they are different" (TLP: 2.0233). The very symbolism of the *Tractatus* has nothing in it to express *kinds* of things. As McGuinness remarked, there are no different "styles of variables according to different kinds of object" (2002: 73). The objectual variable x is in no way restricted by kinds. The existence of kinds would be another hypothesis, one in disagreement with logic, since logic has "no 'subject matter' " (TLP: 6.124). As we have seen, not even specific logical forms like Φxy must exist (TLP: 5.554, 5.5541).[38] Of course, what is not shown in the symbolism cannot be a priori essential.

Thus, what one must realize about the so-called 'ontology' of the *Tractatus* is that the minimal symbolism itself shows it by means of its variables, which allow any form known *a priori* for *whatever* facts. It is meant to pave the way for us to see that the generality of logic is the generality of schematic variables, of what is shown in the symbolism, and not the generality of descriptive propositions that are maximally general (TLP: 6.111). The minimal ontology

---

[38] Variables operating according to kinds of words is an idea that Wittgenstein introduced in 1929–30 only *because* he thought that the project of the *Tractatus* failed (LC: 25). Logical forms that grounded forms of propositions in the *Tractatus* were insufficient to deal with the variety of forms of ordinary language (see RLF). In 1929, Wittgenstein had to complement his old symbolism, precisely because he had to change his views on this topic (Engelmann 2017).

could be expressed by "something exists," i.e., an *a priori* indeterminate number of objects. This boils down to the following: names might name *any* number of objects and elementary propositions make sense (TLP: 6.124). This is like saying "there are facts," which is not expressible in the symbolism as a proposition, but is shown once one understands that propositions will have some logical form and that objectual variables will have some reference.

Still, one might think that the objects of the *Tractatus* are metaphysically fundamental because Wittgenstein suggests the following:

> Things are independent in so far as they can occur in all *possible* situations [*Sachlagen*], but this form of independence is a form of connexion with state of affairs, a form of dependence. (It is impossible for words to appear in different roles: by themselves, and in propositions.) (TLP: 2.0122)

Although Wittgenstein clearly indicates in the parentheses that the talk about objects is meant to be understood as equivalent to the context of words and sentences, one might still be inclined to take objects as determining possibilities of names because of the apparent restriction used by Wittgenstein concerning "*possible* situations." This seems to suggest that there are "impossible situations" that must be ruled out by specific forms or kinds of objects. We have seen above that this is not the case, for specific forms are absent in the *Tractatus*, and forms simply depend on the number of variables (objects). Moreover, there is only logical necessity, i.e., tautological necessity (TLP: 6.37).

A subtlety might help us further with TLP 2.0122. What are the possible *situations (Sachlagen)*? Wittgenstein uses three different words to talk about what one usually would call facts: *Sachverhalt* (state of affairs), *Tatsache* (fact), and *Sachlage* (situation). Unfortunately, he only clearly specifies state of affairs and fact in a letter to Russell from 1919:

> Sachverhalt is, what corresponds to an Elementarsatz if it is true. Tatsache is, what corresponds to a logical product of elementary prop[osition]s when this product is true. (WC: 98)

Of course, the logical precedence of *Satz* in relation to formal concepts related to the world is again clear, for they are understood by means of formal properties of propositions. What are situations and possible/impossible situations, if a *Tatsache* is what corresponds to a "logical product" (conjunction)? In spite of some obscurities concerning 'situation,' one can well understand what Wittgenstein means. *Tatsache* and *Sachverhalt* do not exhaust the parallel between descriptive *Sätze* and facts. Clearly, if facts parallel the true product of elementary propositions (existing state of affairs), they cannot be possible, impossible or necessary, whereas situations can. Situations are what parallel propositions of any complexity, including the essential non-correspondence to facts of tautologies (necessary) and contradictions (impossible). Thus, 'situation' is a notion broader than 'fact,' and it makes reference to the entire logical space (TLP: 2.11, 2.202–3). For instance, situations correspond to the sixteen possible ways in which two elementary propositions can be projected into the world (TLP: 5.101). This is why Wittgenstein says:

> The certainty, possibility, or impossibility of a *situation* [*Sachlage*] is not expressed by a proposition, but by an expression's being a tautology, a proposition with a sense, or a contradiction. (TLP: 5.525, my emphasis)

What, therefore, expresses the "impossibility of a situation" is a formal contradiction, and not the intrinsic combinatorial possibilities of objects. Thus, object x appears in an impossible situation like $\sim((\exists x)\ Fx \rightarrow (\exists x)\ Fx)$ and in the certain or necessary situation $(\exists x)\ (\sim Fx \vee Fx)$. Thus, a possible situation is expressed by any complex proposition that is contingent, but not certain or impossible. This also explains how "objects contain the possibility of all situations" (TLP: 2.014). Any name a, b, or c that takes the place of x in Fx will show the same possible situations, since the complex combinations of Fa and Fb are the same. Either Fa or Fb combined with a proposition Gc, for instance, will generate fourteen possible situations plus tautology and contradiction. Specific objects/names do not create new possibilities and impossibilities. Thus, the prototype x in Fx contains the possibility of all situations: "wherever there is compositeness, argument and function are present, and where these are present, we already have all the logical constants" (TLP: 5.47). This expresses a feature of the general form of propositions and the formal unity of language (Sections 3.1–3).

That logic accounts a priori for any world is not always clear from Wittgenstein's wartime notebooks. This has led interpreters to discuss the nature of simple objects: whether they are sense-data, like Russell's objects of acquaintance (Hintikka & Hintikka, 1986: 45–86), or Hertzian material points (Grasshoff, 1997). Here, one should distinguish two of Wittgenstein's concerns on his way to the *Tractatus*. One was to show the absolutely a priori character of logic, and the other was the analysis of propositions in our actual language. In order to deal with the latter, Wittgenstein considered hypothetical analyses related to the visual field (NB: 64) and to material points in physics (NB: 69, 82). In fact, in the *Prototractatus* the latter kind of analysis is *suggested* when Wittgenstein mentions "the material point with the infinite space around it" (PT: 2.0141). However, this passage does not end up in the *Tractatus* exactly because there cannot be a hypothesis in a priori logic. Wittgenstein coherently foregoes any indication of hypotheses about the actual analysis of our ordinary language, the "application of logic" (TLP: 5.557).

3 Ladder Lessons 1: Formal Unity, Symbolism, and No Self-Defeat

3.1 Understanding the Author and Climbing 'Equivalents'

Although "understanding the author" has been deemed fundamental, arguably interpreters have not paid attention to an essential authorial feature of the *Tractatus*, that is the construction of a ladder *by means of* a numbering system.[39] Ficker asked Wittgenstein whether the *Tractatus* could be published without the numbers of the sentences.[40] In a letter from December 1919, Wittgenstein replied that numbers "absolutely must be printed alongside" the sentences, for the book would be an "incomprehensible jumble" without them (von Wright, 1980: 87). Moreover, *only* the numbering system would give "perspicuity [*Übersichtlichkeit*] and clarity" to the book (von Wright, 1980: 86–7; my translation). We must understand, therefore, *how* the author intended one to climb the *whole* "ladder" according to a numbering system that he invented in order to give perspicuity and clarity to the book.

We begin with how the "rungs" of the ladder are connected, for the numbering displayed in major remarks (TLP 1–7) instructs us *how* to read the book (not the "frame"). This can be seen in an *übersichtliche*, or a bird's eye view, presentation of the most important sentences of the book and its central concepts either underlined or italicized:

1. The world is everything that *is the case.*
2. What *is the case*, the fact, is the existence of atomic facts.
3. The logical picture of the facts is the *thought.*
4. The *thought* is the significant proposition.
5. Propositions are *truth-functions* of elementary propositions.
6. The general form of *truth-functions* is: $[\bar{p}, \bar{\xi}, N(\bar{\xi})]$.
7. What we cannot speak about we must pass over in silence.

According to the sole footnote of the *Tractatus*, introduced on its first page, *all* other sentences of the book are, directly or indirectly, remarks on 1, 2, 3, 4, 5, or 6, since the "logical importance" of all other sentences is subordinated to them (TLP 7 is the result of the book). What is the point of the most important sentences and their sequence? Each major sentence from 1 to 6 presents two major formal concepts that work like vertical side rails that sustain and connect the rungs by means of informal definitions, but one concept, of course, is the central one. Recall that when Wittgenstein solidified the method of the

---

[39] Bazzocchi (2015) has insisted on the significance of the numbering system and its "tree" structure for the correct understanding of particularities of the *Tractatus*. However, it is even more significant for the point of the book as a whole.

[40] Ideas presented in this section were introduced in Engelmann (2013) and (2018b).

Tractatus, he claimed that his "*whole* task is to explain the nature of *Satz* [sentence/proposition]" (NB: 39; my translation). Indeed, the very ladder of the book shows in an *übersichtliche* way that it is *Satz* that gives it unity, as the parallels between thoughts and propositions, atomic facts and elementary propositions, and world and the general form of propositions indicate.

The significance of "*Satz*" is expressed by the sequence of numbers of the ladder structure. They indicate that we move from the *lowest* (TLP: 1) to the *highest* (TLP: 6) rung of the ladder before we reach TLP 7. The move from 2 to 3 shows that there is no way of reaching up to the *essence* of facts except by means of their "logical picture." What matters for logic concerning facts is the logical modelling of facts, i.e., the sentence (*Satz*), as the passage from 3 to 4 makes clear. With this movement, and with the parallels between proposition, thought, and fact, Wittgenstein wants to indicate that the essence of *Satz* gives the clue for the essence of thought and world. In the *Philosophical Investigations*, he explains the crucial point beginning at the highest rung: "proposition, language, thought, world, stand in line one behind the other, each *equivalent* to each" (PI: §96). They are all "in a certain sense one" (TLP 4.014). The world is facts; facts are given as pictured in thoughts, which are sentences, which have a purely logical essence. The sequence of "rung" definitions that we are meant to climb give us a way to see anew and to gradually *replace* obscure notions expressed in words by the *equivalent* "absolutely simple" and "as clear as crystal" central piece of the *symbolism* of the book: the general form of propositions (PI: §97). 'World,' 'fact,' and 'thought' are formal concepts and, therefore, should be "represented in the notation by variables" (TLP: 4.1272). However, since these formal concepts do not appear in the symbolism itself as variables or anything else, one must understand that they are 'equivalents' of what is shown in the symbolism with the general form of propositions. Therefore, the task of giving "the nature of the proposition" coincides with the task of "giving the nature of all facts" (NB: 39). In the transition of equivalents, the essence of the world, thought, and language is expressed in *[p̄, ξ̄, N(ξ̄)]*, for to give *the general form of propositions* is to give "the essence of all description, *and thus the essence of the world*" (TLP: 5.4711; my emphasis). This essence includes tautologies expressed by the general form (Sections 3.4–3.5).

The general form at the top of the ladder also shows what we can leave behind, or throw away. In the first moment, the *talk* about formal concepts such as 'world,' 'fact,' 'object' is replaced by the talk about 'thought,' 'language,' and 'totality of propositions,' 'proposition,' and 'objectual variable.' This is a first replacement of 'equivalents.' However, on the way up the ladder, we must give up not only nonsensical sentences about the world, such as "the world is the totality of facts" (TLP: 1.1), but also about language, such as "the totality of propositions is language" (TLP: 4.001). The talk about sentences or signs is as nonsensical as the talk about facts, objects, or thoughts. Thus, these formal concepts are left behind as well. They must disappear and give place to variables expressing pure forms. Ultimately, they are replaced by a purely formal *symbolic* presentation that takes the place of 'language,' 'sentence,' and 'objectual variable.' Thus, the number system gives "perspicuity and clarity," as Wittgenstein told Ficker, because one sees things clearly if one sees things logically, i.e., by means of a perspicuous symbolism that characterizes the right logical point of view. We see it at the highest rung of the major remarks (TLP: 6) before the ladder is thrown away and silence demanded (TLP: 7). The general form of propositions itself is not nonsensical, and we can keep it. Once we grasp it, we can see what happens to philosophical problems in TLP 6.1n–6.5n (I discuss this in Sections 4.1–4.5).

The final lesson that the *Tractatus* lays down with the ladder structure is that philosophy can only express the essence of anything if it understands that essence is strictly formal (*shown*). Thus, the essence of 'the world' or 'the thought' is not really *explained* or even asserted. We do not grasp or ground essence by means of sentences. Actually, essence is grasped only if we give up asserting and grounding, and accept that it is shown in the empty general form of propositions, the form of language. 'Essence' is expressed in logic, it is *shown* in purely formal terms (TLP: 3.34, 4.5, 5.4711, 6.12, 6.124). Therefore, the ladder structure of the book gives expression to the insight that if we want to grasp the essence of world and thought, *all* we really get is an empty form that shows the essence of propositions. In philosophy, we say nothing.

Therefore, the very formulation of the question concerning the essence of the world is a "misunderstanding of the logic of language" (TLP: preface), for it makes us expect a proposition describing a hitherto unknown feature of reality, while all philosophy can do is to display the essence of reality with a perspicuous symbolism that does not say anything (it shows). Thus, Russell's philosophical propositions, which should be completely general and a priori, neither proved nor disproved by experience (Russell, 1914b: 85–6), will disappear. The generality of the logic of language and world is schematic, and by means of free variables and rules it expresses only what is strictly formal, empty of any content. Russell's "general aspects of the world" (Russell, 1914a: 28), correctly understood, are formal. "Saying nothing," although not satisfying for Russell and other philosophers (TLP: 6.54), is all one can get. 'Scientific philosophy' will not discover "ultimate metaphysical truth" (Russell, 1914a: 40) simply because the 'ultimate truth' is empty, purely formal, and not a yet unknown feature of reality. We will see in Sections 4.1–4.5 how this idea extends to the problems of philosophy in general.

3.2 Symbolism: The Formal Unity of Language

The solution of philosophical problems "in essentials" is really the introduction of a formal solution in order to overcome traditional philosophy and its questioning, which makes us expect the wrong kind of answer. The solution consists in expressing the "logic of our language" (TLP: preface) in its formal unity, where we see what we already know *a priori*. As we saw in Section 2.3, Wittgenstein's investigative method is "not to sunder the hard from the soft, but to see the hardness of the soft" (NB: 44). Since his "*whole* task consists in explaining the nature of the sentence [*Satz*]" (NB: 39), we must see the hard in the nature of sentences when we study sign-languages (TLP: 4.112). In order to do so, the distinction between two groups of rules employed in descriptions of facts should be observed: non-arbitrary and arbitrary rules. The "decisive point" is that "some things are arbitrary in the symbols," and some are not, but in logic only the non-arbitrary finds expression (TLP: 6.124). What is non-arbitrarily determined is fundamentally what is essential to the rules that structure what "follows logically," the rules of what is not arbitrary (NM: 114; cf. TLP: 3.342), which is the fundamental expression of the a priori essence of language, the "hard." The hard is expressed by what is essential in ordinary propositions, i.e., features that "alone enable the proposition to express its sense" (TLP: 3.34).

Wittgenstein's symbolism "in which everything is all right" (TLP: 4.1213) presents the essence of language, the "hard," in its formal unity, as "the logic of our language" (TLP: preface).[41] In spite of some ambiguities, Wittgenstein uses the following synonymously: 'symbolism' (TLP: 4.31, 4.4611, 5.452), 'notation' (*Notation*) (TLP: 3.342, 5.474, 5.512, 5.514, 6.1203, 6.122, 6.123), 'sign language' (*Zeichensprache*) (TLP: 3.325, 3.343, 4.1121, 4.1213, 6.124), and 'system of signs' (TLP: 5.475, 5.555).[42] Moreover, he equates symbolism and *Begriffsschrift* (TLP: 3.325, 4.1272, 4.1273, 4.431, 5.533, and 5.334).[43] *Begriffsschrift* ('conceptual notation') is meant to include the entire symbolism. There are notational devices that are part of it. Wittgenstein says that he wants to eliminate identity from "our notation" and this will take place by means of a specific notation (NB: 33–4). Thus, in the *Tractatus*, he says, "the sign of identity, therefore, is not an essential constituent of *the* conceptual notation [*der Begriffsschrift*]" (TLP: 5.533; my translation and emphasis).

---

[41] Obviously, the fundamental role of the symbolism in philosophy is derived from Frege's *Begriffsschrift*. However, the role of symbolisms is also fundamental in the philosophy of physics of Boltzmann and Hertz, who are important influences. See Engelmann (2018b).

[42] In a letter to Ogden, he explicitly asks him to translate *Zeichensprache* as symbolism (LO: 25).

[43] When Wittgenstein discusses the translation of 5.5563 with Ogden, he talks about "propositions written down, say, in Russell's symbolism or any other 'Begriffsschrift' " (LO: 50).

The symbolism is in many ways inherited from Frege and Russell, but Wittgenstein introduces new notations (the general form and truth tables) and eliminates some, for instance identity (Section 2.5). What underlies the permanence of some notations, and the introduction and elimination of others, is a quest for the formal unity of language expressing all that we know a priori – the hard – concerning the logic of our language.

3.3 Prototype

The basic piece of notation is function and argument (TLP: 3.31n). Wittgenstein subordinates that idea, inherited from Frege and Russell, to his own project of showing the formal unity of language (Section 3.4). Many ordinary sentences appear as sentences that are not composed of connectives and quantifiers, with the same possible forms as elementary propositions (more on this below). Those sentences have a "logical prototype":

> If we turn a constituent of a proposition into a variable, there is a class of propositions all of which are values of the resulting variable proposition. In general, this class too will be dependent on *the meaning that our arbitrary conventions have given to parts of the original proposition*. But if all the signs in it that have arbitrarily determined meanings are turned into *variables*, we shall still get a class of this kind. This one, however, is *not dependent on any convention*, but *solely on the nature* of the proposition. It corresponds to a logical form – a logical prototype [*Urbild*]. (TLP: 3.315; my emphasis)

The "logical prototype" is free from what is "arbitrarily determined." Only the meanings of "parts of the original proposition" are determined arbitrarily. The prototype is "dependent . . . solely on the nature of the proposition" because it is given *a priori*:

> We portray the thing, the relation, the property, by means of *variables* and *so shew* that we do not derive these ideas from particular cases that occur to us, but possess them somehow *a priori*. (NB: 65; my emphasis)

One knows that one possesses the prototype a priori because of the role of variables in portraying things, properties, and relations. Real (free) variables operating schematically express a generality different in nature from the generality expressed by quantifiers. It is essential generality, which is purely formal and non-arbitrary, in contrast to accidental generality (TLP: 6.124). The generality of 'any' is not assertive (it shows), and appears in schematic form, while the generality of 'all' is assertive, and expressed in general propositions. As structuring forms operating schematically, prototypes are not derived from anything, but are present "somehow a priori." In this way, we can think of φx or $\varphi xy,$ etc., as each being a "particular prototype" (NB: 46). However, we do not know a priori the real particular prototypes, the specific forms, of elementary propositions (TLP: 5.5541) – see Section 2.6.

According to Wittgenstein, "in the proposition we hold a prototype [*Urbild*] up against reality" (NB: 32; modified translation). This means that the prototype is implicitly present in sentences: "The fact that there is no sign for a particular prototype [*Urbild*] does not show that that prototype is not present" (NB: 46; modified translation). A prototype is not a thing, but an implicit determinant of the structuring traits of propositions. It displays the general rules that ground "internal relations" of words and objects or sets of objects:

> "a" *can* go proxy for a and "b" *can* go proxy for b when "a" stands in the relation "R" to "b"; this is what the POTENTIAL internal relation that we are looking for consists in. (NB: 41)

Potential internal relations grounded in the prototype simply indicate the structuring possibilities that determine a projection in language, a structure of a picture (TLP: 2.15). In projections, internal relations are grounded in the a priori prototype, which is the "logical pattern" that constitutes projections of sentences into the world (TLP: 4.014). So a logical pattern, a prototype, determines projections by means of structuring rules in a picturing relation. After indicating that an "internal relation" holds between language and world in TLP 4.014, Wittgenstein explains the idea in the following sentence:

> There is a *general rule* by means of which the musician can obtain the symphony from the score [...] That is what constitutes the inner similarity between these things [...] And *that rule is the law of projection* [...] It is *the rule* for translating this language . (TLP: 4.0141; all emphases mine)

Rules that constitute the inner similarity depend on the "logical pattern," the prototype, but they always work with arbitrarily determined rules that we have made in the use of sentences (names we give, potential relations that we ascribe, etc.). Arbitrarily determined rules of a projection allow us to depict facts and to present possible facts (*abbilden* and *darstellen*). The logical structure is just the same in both cases.

Whereas the prototype structures projected sentences, it also restricts projections. It guarantees that although names and relations are arbitrarily fixed, the sentence itself is not, for the prototype gives its structuring rules in context. What is not in accord with the rules grounded in the a priori prototype and in arbitrarily determined rules in use is not a projection at all. Here is an example:

> The reason why, e.g., it seems as if "Plato Socrates" might have a meaning, while "Abracadabra Socrates" will never be suspected to have one, is because we know that "Plato" has one, and do not observe that in order that the whole

> phrase should have one, what is necessary is *not* that "Plato" should have one, but that the fact *that* "Plato" is *to the left of a name* should. (NM: 116)

It might *seem* that "Plato Socrates" has meaning because in some contexts 'Plato' is meaningful (for instance, "Plato is wise"). This is not enough. In order to project a sentence that can be compared with reality, a model (*Bild*), we need to use the symbols function and argument that express "POTENTIAL internal relations" (NB: 41) *together*, contextually, with arbitrary rules that we give. The employment of those symbols by means of arbitrary rules determines the projection of a fact by means of a fact in language (TLP: 3.14n). Following Ricketts, we can say that two kinds of rules must work together: rules of designation and rules of agreement of form (1996: 74). The fact that Plato is wise, for instance, is represented by the fact *that* the word 'Plato' appears to the left of the propositional function 'x is F' – an expression of the particular prototype – together with the specific arbitrarily determined rules of language, for instance that 'Plato' means Plato. Therefore, in a sentence like "Plato is wise," an arbitrary rule determines the meaning of a name and another rule determines a structuring predicate. Thus, what is wrong with "Plato Socrates" is that we have given no arbitrarily determined rule that allows the name 'Plato' to stand to the left of another name. This is not one of the rules "that we give" (NM: 114). In this case, we lack "the meaning that our arbitrary conventions have given to parts of the [...] proposition" (TLP: 3.315; quoted above).

Note that arbitrarily determined rules are binding. We are committed to them, since they are fixed by our ordinary use of language structured by the a priori prototype. This is the reason why ordinary rules of projection are "internal relations" (TLP: 4.014-1) and why we have to pay attention to the "significant use" (TLP: 3.326).

Thus, as argued by Diamond (see Section 1.2), we do not investigate whether there is a clash of categories in order to determine that "Socrates is identical" is nonsense. It is nonsense because we have given no meaning to 'identical' as an adjective, and not because we are doing something impossible by combining what cannot be combined (TLP: 5.4733). However, this does not mean that we need a piecemeal investigation in order to find out whether "Socrates is identical" means anything, as resolute readers claim. The binding character of rules that we give indicates that a specific investigation of what is finally meant by words is not needed in order to point out that such a string of words is nonsensical. The lack of an arbitrarily determined rule concerning 'x is identical' is enough to classify "Socrates is identical" as nonsense. Philosophers have to follow, as does everybody else, arbitrarily determined rules of language as well as a priori rules of logic. Even if they invent "new uses," they must go back to arbitrarily determined rules in order to explain them (Engelmann 2018a).

The fact that words have meaning in pictures or models (*Bilder*) coincides with sentences being bipolar. For when a picture (*Bild*) can be true and can be false, rules for the prototype together with arbitrarily determined rules have been projected: "the being true or false actually *constitutes* the relation of the proposition to reality" (NM: 113; my emphasis; cf. TLP: 5.4733). If no projection takes place (there is no model modelling facts), signs do not express something that can be true and can be false. This is obvious, for in cases like "Socrates is identical" there is no comparison with reality at all. In such cases, bipolarity shows that no further investigation is needed.

However, this does not mean that the final solution of philosophical problems is given by bipolarity. Classifying sentences as 'nonsensical' does not solve philosophical problems. The nonsense surrounding philosophical questioning has a different ground, as indicated in Section 3.1. I return to this in Section 4.

3.4 The Unity of the Prototype and Complex Forms

Very often, ordinary sentences conceal elementary ones and logical symbols, particularly because ordinary names hide definite descriptions. In these cases, what we have in place are "tacit conventions," which can be "enormously complicated" (TLP: 4.003). In complicated cases, forms are "projected by means of a definition into a name" (NB: 69). Of course, it is Russell's analysis of definite descriptions that allows us to see how forms are projected into names and to understand the "real logical form" of a sentence (TLP: 4.0031). A projection defines that "a proposition about a complex stands in internal relation to the proposition about its constituent part" (TLP: 3.24). If forms are projected by means of definition (an internal relation) into a name, then we have a guarantee that "this name can then also be treated as a real one" (NB: 69). Like a "real name," the name 'Socrates,' which has "forms projected by means of definition into a name," is also used in inferences (NB: 69). Essentially, ordinary sentences work logically like elementary ones. This parallels the idea that possible prototypes for ordinary and elementary propositions are the same: "I write elementary propositions as functions of names, so that they have the form 'fx', $\varphi(x,y)$', etc." (TLP: 4.24).

Although they ground inferences in which ordinary and simple names might appear, prototypes are not sufficient to express the hard ('following logically') in language. Evidently, neither projections of forms into ordinary names, nor quantification, nor logical constants, which are also projected, are expressed by the prototype alone. We still need to see the purely formal unity of what Wittgenstein later called atomic and molecular logic (LC: 252). Grounded of course in function and argument, one sees what needs unification. For instance, any two possible facts *Fa* and *Gb*, both expressions of the prototype *Φx*, can be projected in sixteen situations, all grounded in the possibility of truth and falsehood of sentences and the rules of logical connectives. In such a case, we will have fourteen ways of projection into the world (descriptive sentences) and two empty limiting cases: tautology and contradiction. Of course, this is shown in truth tables by means of propositional variables *p* and *q* (TLP: 4.31, 5.101). Similarly, if we project quantification, we need function and argument prototypes in order to say that some, all, etc., objects are related by means of certain predicates and relations.

The overall logical unity of language and its limits is given by means of the general form of propositions, for it expresses the complexity of possible projections, including tautology and contradiction. It works with the basis of the logical prototype and rules for the construction of molecular propositions. Note, "the general propositional form is a variable" (TLP: 4.53). The operation varies over what the propositional variables (propositional functions) determine (TLP: 5.501). Thus, in the general form of the proposition it is assumed that the logical prototype expresses the possible forms of elementary propositions: *Φx*, *Φxy*, etc. (TLP: 4.24). We do not know a priori which *specific* forms will be found in analysis, but we do know the *possible* forms, since we know how to operate with the prototypes (TLP: 5.555). If we did not know that, we would not be able to foresee some propositional forms, and it would be incorrect to say "there cannot be a proposition whose form could not have been foreseen (i.e., constructed)" (TLP: 4.5). The general propositional form shows, in its turn, that by means of the operation *N* operating in accordance with the prototype, all complex forms can be constructed (TLP: 6). An operation, Wittgenstein writes, is "that according to which signs can be constructed *according to a rule*" (NB: 90; my emphasis). The introduction of the rule *N*, then, signalizes that all essential elements of the form of any sentence are unified: the general form concludes the presentation of the formal unity of language. That is why it is placed at the top of the ladder (Section 3.1).

The unity is shown, in principle, by the very elucidation of *N*, which negates one proposition or many simultaneously (TLP: 5.51). Thus N(Fa)= ~Fa and N(Fa, Fb)= ~Fa ∧ ~Fb express truth tables such that (F,T) and (F,F,F,T) respectively, i.e., (—T). ~(∃x) Fx is simply a negation like (~Fa ∧ ~Fb ...), which is also a variation on (—T) (TLP: 5.5, 5.501–2; 5.52). Thus, quantification is constructed by a rule (operation) *N* applied to functions like Fx (TLP: 5.501).[44] This assumes that quantification works grounded in a limiting case. In (F,F,F, ..., T), 'T' expresses what would be the last line of a truth table. If this is correct, tautological inferences involving quantification are expressible in

---

[44] Floyd (2001) presents a detailed account of quantification in the *Tractatus*.

truth tables: (x) ~Fx → ~Fa would be (~Fa ∧ ~Fb ∧ ~Fc ...) → ~Fa.[45] Therefore, "the fact that '$(x).fx{:}\supset{:}fa$' is a tautology shows that fa follows from '$(x).fx$' " (TLP: 6.1201). That tautologies are connected with the general form of propositions is relevant, for they show symbolically "the formal – logical – properties of language *and the world*" (TLP: 6.12; my emphasis) – see Section 3.1.

The general form also generates the propositional calculus and its tautologies. Since N(p, q) is ~p ∧ ~q, one can see, for instance, that p ∨ q would be N(N(p,q)), and so on. The cases of empty "logical laws" and contradictions that say nothing can also be constructed. For instance, one might construct a contradiction as follows. Since N(p)= ~p and N(p, q)= ~p ∧ ~q (TLP: 5.51), we have N(N(p), p)= ~~p ∧ ~p. Of course, N applied to the whole again gives us a tautology. In this way, the hard, i.e., what follows logically and its grounds, is completely shown in the symbolism, for supposedly inferences have ultimately a tautological character (TLP: 6.1201) – I return to this below.

3.5 The Showing Symbolism Dissolves the Appearance of Self-Defeat

The symbolism presents the "hard" in language as free from anything arbitrarily determined in our use of signs. The logical prototype, truth tables, and the operation *N* are symbolic expressions of what is given *a priori* as necessary signs (TLP: 6.124). This is Wittgenstein's way of expressing the nature or essence of proposition and language (TLP: 3.334, 3.343–41, 5.476, 5.512–4). The essential, the "hard," is what is shown in the symbolism, and "once we have *a symbolism* in which everything is all right, *we already have the correct logical point of view*" (TLP: 4.1213; modified translation; my emphasis).

"The correct logical point of view" expressed in the "symbolism in which everything is all right" is the point of view from which we see "the world aright" (TLP: 6.54). Nothing more is required, for the symbolism expresses the unity of the "logic of our language" (TLP: preface). Once we have grasped it, we have reached the point "in which the answers to questions are symmetrically combined – *a priori* – to form a self-contained system" (TLP: 5.4541). Here, as Wittgenstein explains later in *Philosophical Investigations*, we have found "the *hardest* thing there is," the "*utterly simple*" (PI: §97). We have made clear "a realm subject to the law: *Simplex sigillum veri*" (TLP: 5.4541). That is, we have found the "truth itself *in its entirety*" (TLP: 5.5563; emphasis added).

---

[45] This assumes "dots of laziness," an assumption that Wittgenstein later considered mistaken (LC: 217).

In order to dissolve the appearance of self-defeat that inevitably seems to be generated by the fact that Wittgenstein calls the sentences of the book 'nonsensical' (TLP: 6.54), one must understand that, in principle, the symbolism standing alone is enough for us to see "the world aright" (TLP: 6.54). After all, it alone presents the hardness of the soft in language, i.e., "the logic of our language" (TLP: preface, 4.003). Therefore, if one understands it, one understands the limits that it draws in language (TLP: preface). The very sentences of the *Tractatus* are, therefore, dispensable nonsense that we overcome, as the very ladder structure suggests and the position of the general form of the proposition makes clear (Section 3.1).

What makes the symbolism self-standing is the fact that it does not say anything, but only shows the formal unity of language. The point of 'showing' is that neither variables, nor the operation N purport to present truths of any sort. They only give rules of language that ultimately make explanatory sentences dispensable. In what follows, I look at the showing notations of the *Tractatus* and how they do this work.

As we have seen above, a prototype like φx is just an empty schematic form that is expressed by real variables. It says nothing and merely indicates what is a priori in language. It makes no sense to say that φx is true. One cannot affirm or deny such a prototype, and one cannot take it as nonsense either, since it is an empty form. It simply gives the a priori formal rules that we already use implicitly in ordinary projections.

Truth tables, similarly, do not affirm or deny anything, but show formal structures among sentences. Consider:

p	q	p ∧ q	p ∨ q	(p ∧ q) → (p ∨ q)
T	T	T	T	T
T	F	F	T	T
F	T	F	T	T
F	F	F	F	T

Truth tables always present schematic variables that indicate that any sentence can take their *place*. Variables p, q, etc., do not assert anything. The first two columns show all the possibilities of how those propositions can be constructed. Again, nothing is asserted, but all possibilities are displayed. What $p \wedge q$ shows is, as Wittgenstein put it later, "the essence of 'and' " (LC: 60). It is a complete formal description of the meaning of 'and.'[46] As such, it

---

[46] However, on his return to philosophy in 1929, Wittgenstein abandoned such a view. See Engelmann 2018c.

does not say anything, but it expresses formal properties by means of two variables and the rules of projection for the connective. The connective stands for nothing in the world, since it merely projects the truth possibilities given under sentences that take the place of 'p' and 'q.'

The schematic presentation above also shows how "every tautology itself shows that it is a tautology" (TLP: 6.127). The tautology above shows that a sentence of the form 'p ∨ q' follows from 'p ∧ q,' for, given all truth possibilities, it is impossible for the former to be false when the latter is true (see TLP: 6.1201). The tautology also shows that logical laws do not say anything, for its truth-value remains the same – it does not matter what real sentences replace the variables *and* what happens in the world (as shown by the left columns of Ts and Fs). That is, the specific senses of the sentences and their truth-values are irrelevant for a tautology. Thus, it is clear that our inferences do not depend on any facts, and are completely formal and absolutely necessary.

In the general form of the proposition, the N operator says nothing, but "shows itself in a variable; it shows how we can proceed from one form of proposition to another" (TLP-OT: 5.24). It indicates a possible procedure of construction. Only the result of an application of the rule N to real sentences (not to variables that appear in the form) says something (TLP: 5.25).

Finally, Wittgenstein's notation for the elimination of identity, essentially, introduces rules for how one notation is replaced by another (TLP: 5.53n). As seen in Section 2.5, Wittgenstein had good reasons not to accept Russell's theory of identity. In accordance with that, the notation of the *Tractatus* shows the dispensability of identity. Identity is clearly superfluous, since " 'fa' says the same as '$(\exists x).fx.x =a$' " (TLP: 5.47). The "disappearance" of identity can be extended to all relevant cases with some rules. We can express identity of objects, i.e., the fact that we are talking about the same object on different occasions, by means of identity of signs, and difference of objects by a difference in signs. Thus, instead of writing 'f(a,b) ∧ a=b,' which "disappears" from the notation, one simply writes 'f(a,a),' etc. (TLP: 5.531). The same rule then applies to quantified propositions (TLP: 5.532). Thus, instead of writing Russell's uniqueness condition in definite descriptions as "$(\exists x) ((Fx \wedge (y) (Fy \rightarrow x=y))$)," one writes "$(\exists x) Fx \wedge \sim(\exists x,y) Fx \wedge Fy$." Wittgenstein's notation simply replaces Russell's, translates it, and preserves the idea of analysis of definite descriptions and ordinary names behind it. This is relevant, as seen in Section 2.5, because Russell's definition helps show "*how* language takes care of itself" (NB: 43).

The entire logical symbolism of the *Tractatus* is, then, an articulation of a priori rules that do not assert anything, but display schematically the unity of the structure of language. Considering that the formal rules of logic enable us to foresee the form of any proposition and determine the formal limits of language, the *Tractatus* is not self-defeating or paradoxical when Wittgenstein calls his sentences nonsensical (*unsinnig*) (TLP: 6.54). Of course, those sentences of the *Tractatus* that cannot be written in the symbolism are nonsense, but they are not identical with the rules of the self-standing logical symbolism (notations) of the book. Thus, in a sense "understanding the author" means understanding how the book is to be read grounded in its ladder structure and its symbolism, for both indicate why and how one throws away the nonsense. One must overcome the sentences of the book and throw away the nonsense once one understands the formal unity of "the logic of our language" (TLP: preface, 4.003). As we saw in Section 3.1, this point is displayed in the numbering system of the book, which indicates how it is to be read.

Therefore, the logical symbolism itself *shows* the logic of our language and precludes self-defeat in the *Tractatus*. This is why Wittgenstein calls the notion of 'showing' the "cardinal problem of philosophy" in a letter to Russell (WC: 98). 'Showing' grounds the explicitation of the hardness of the soft, as argued above. In a previous letter, Russell agreed that logical propositions are tautologies (WC: 96). Wittgenstein, however, added that the case of tautologies was "only a corollary" (WC: 98) of the saying/showing distinction. As seen above, tautologies are just a *case* among many of what is generally shown, for what is shown is the entire logical symbolism, the essence of logic, which cannot say anything. That is the guiding insight (or logical doctrine) presupposed in the book.

The nonsensical sentences of the *Tractatus* from 1.n to 6 help us to grasp the symbolism. The movement from 6 to 7 shows us its philosophical results (I discuss these in the next section). However, it might seem paradoxical that nonsensical sentences can be helpful at all. In order to dissolve this appearance of paradox, we should not forget some aspects of nonsensical sentences in the *Tractatus*. First, they do not show; it is the symbolism that shows. This is why the notion of 'showing' itself is "cardinal." In principle, we could grasp just the symbolism alone without the help of the sentences of the book. Second, the sentences of the book do not explain or give an argument for why sentences of the book are nonsense. The ground for the nonsensicality of sentences of the book is just the symbolism that shows itself. Nothing more is required. Those sentences themselves are neither descriptions of facts, nor necessary propositions of logic, nor any other kind of expression of the formal properties of language (see Sections 4.1–4.5). This point is also suggested and in agreement with the very ladder structure (Section 3.1). Third, if one understands the logical symbolism that shows itself, and understands that it is self-standing, the elucidations of the book are ultimately superfluous, redundant, 'tautologous' remarks. One should understand it, for it merely shows clearly the structure (the "hardness") of a language that one already understands, if one has learned to speak (Rhees, 1970: 10, 47). Thus, in principle, elucidations are dispensable. In his dictations to Moore in 1914, Wittgenstein argues "That M is a thing can't be *said*; it is nonsense" (NM: 109). However, it is nonsense as something "superfluous, tautologous" (NM: 110). Of course, the symbolism itself eliminates an expression like "M is a thing" by showing that 'thing' is expressed by an argument variable and not by a predicate (TLP: 4.1211, 4.126). Wittgenstein's use of 'tautology' as a superfluous remark appears also in the *Notebooks*: "Is it a tautology to say: *Language* consists of *sentences*? It seems it *is*" (NB: 52). In the *Tractatus,* one finds the sentence "the totality of propositions is language" (TLP: 4.001). It is a 'tautology' made superfluous by the general form of propositions. Fourth, as superfluous remarks, nonsensical sentences of the book are neither 'truths' nor 'metaphysical necessities,' but simply remarks that one overcomes after one grasps the logical symbolism and how the book is to be read. The superfluous remarks are *like* tautologies in that they are empty of content and say nothing, but they are not (real) logical tautologies, for they are not part of the symbolism that displays the formal unity of the logic of language. By calling them nonsense, Wittgenstein makes clear that tautologous redundant remarks are not metaphysical necessities.

4 Ladder Lessons 2: Problems of Philosophy Solved in Essentials

4.1 Bipolarity as a Logical Distinction

It is tempting to think that the *Tractatus* gives a *sui generis* definition of the proposition as something that is bipolar. One might call this the basis for a theory of meaning. From bipolarity, then, one would conclude that metaphysical sentences are nonsense and, thus, that philosophical problems have been solved. However, one should resist this temptation. Such a reductive definition would not be a good ground, for it is not clear that metaphysicians ever wanted to defend or justify bipolar sentences. Moreover, if a principle alone, whose justification is unclear, has such consequences, one might well say 'So much worse for that principle' (McManus 2010: 59). In any case, such a *sui generis* definition would not show how philosophical problems are solved "in essentials" (TLP: preface).

However, Wittgenstein did not regard metaphysical sentences as nonsense simply because they are not bipolar. He presented a series of fruitful and complex argumentative moves that are meant to bring us to a new, formal, view of philosophy. There are kinds of *Satz*. The point of *departure* is the elucidation of *one* kind of *Satz*, namely sentences that model or depict facts called pictures or models (*Bilder*) (TLP: 2.1n). Since we compare pictures or models with reality, they are bipolar, i.e., they *can* be true *and* they *can* be false (TLP: 2.1n, 4.01n). Even *if* there are sentences that *are* simply true or false (say, principles of science, mathematics, logic, and ethics), they are still logically different from sentences that *can* be true and can be false.

This non-reductionist point of departure is particularly relevant because both Russell and Frege neglected the specificity of propositions that work like models or pictures when they gave a general characterization of propositions as something that *is* true or false. Thus, their characterization of thought and proposition as expressions of all kinds of propositions was misleading. It masked an important and undeniable *logical* distinction.[47] Their *symbolisms* do not capture it.

With *Satz* as *Bild* Wittgenstein simply draws and emphasizes a fundamental distinction in logic. He does not thereby introduce a "doctrine" of any kind. In line with Sections 2 and 3, one must notice that the distinction is shown in truth tables, where, except for tautology and contradiction, the formal presentation of any proposition appears with at least one T and one F in the column of possibilities. Thus, bipolarity is intrinsically connected with the essence of logical connectives.

The bipolar *Satz* is also relevant because it guides the understanding of the nature of other kinds of *Satz*. This movement is obvious with logic and the tautological nature of its *Sätze*. However, once the contrast between contingent (bipolar) and necessary (tautological) is given in purely logical terms, the process of elucidation of kinds of *Satz* continues in remarks 6.1n–6.5n. Now the point is that Russell (and Frege) failed to see specificities of sentences of logic, mathematics, science, and Ethics in contrast with the bipolar *Satz* and tautologies.

This elucidation is not a desperate refutation of apparent counter examples to the general form of the proposition, but a brief investigation, in essentials, of the fundamental problems of philosophy grounded in the general form of propositions and kinds of *Satz*. Philosophical problems are many, but the metaphysical question par excellence concerns the nature of reality. The nature of reality is the ultimate essence of any world, something that parallels the essence of logic, of language, and thought. Thus, this question is solved by the general form of the proposition and its position in the "ladder," as already seen in Section 3.1. The very "positing of the question" (*Fragestellung*) (TLP: preface, my translation), as we have seen, is a misunderstanding of the logic of our language, for it makes

---

[47] Since they also assumed that all propositions are about something, they concluded that logical and mathematical objects exist.

us expect an ultimate description, which would reveal the discovery of something new, when we can only present an empty form that expresses (shows) essential rules that do not say anything.

However, other philosophical problems guide and ground the quest for the ultimate essence of reality: Is mathematics reducible to logic? How is a priori mathematics applied to the world? Are the principles of causality and induction a priori true or justified? Can we justify principles of Ethics? What is the essence of value and the meaning of life?, etc. These kinds of problems appear in the group 6.n of remarks, the closing movement of the book, where various kinds of *Satz* are discussed. An overview based on the numbering system gives us the following:

6   The general form of truth-functions is: $[\bar{p}, \bar{\xi}, N(\bar{\xi})]$.

6.1 The propositions of logic are tautologies.

6.2 Mathematics is a logical method. The propositions of mathematics are equations, and therefore pseudo-propositions.

6.3 Logical research means the investigation of *all regularity*. And outside logic everything is accidental.

6.4 All propositions are of equal value.

6.5 For an answer that cannot be expressed the question too cannot be expressed.

The riddle does not exist.

If a question can be put at all, then it *can* also be answered. (TLP-OT)

The handling of various philosophical problems appears after the presentation of the general form of propositions, i.e., after the presentation of the formal unity of the essence of the logic of our language (and any language), in which the contrast between the contingent (bipolar) and the necessary (tautological) *Satz* is clear. The problems appear in a sequence of subjects according to kinds of *Satz*: logic (6.1n), mathematics (6.2n), science (6.3n), ethics and value (6.4n), and the riddle of life (6.5n). The remarks numbered 6.n, then, together with the elucidation of the quest for the essence of the world, must allow us to see why philosophical matters, and particularly how philosophical questioning (*Fragestellung*), "rests on the misunderstanding of the logic of our language" and how "the problems have in essentials been finally solved" (TLP-OT: preface).

The structure of TLP 6.n also indicates an answer to Russell's views on the nature of philosophical questioning presented mostly in *Problems of Philosophy* (1912), a book that Wittgenstein read right after his arrival in Cambridge, and in *Our Knowledge of the External World*, a book that, I take it, Wittgenstein read in 1915 (WC: 79). In *Problems of Philosophy*, a book title that itself suggests Wittgenstein's phrasing in the preface of the *Tractatus*,

Russell discusses the primitive propositions of logic, mathematics, science, ethics, and the limits and value of philosophy. According to Russell, the fundamental problems of philosophy are problems concerning the justification of a priori *true* principles.

In TLP 6.n, Wittgenstein accepts the view that philosophy deals only with what is known a priori, but makes the point that if something is known a priori, it is empty of content. "Primitive propositions" are not true about something, but purely formal. If purely formal, and not properly true, one should not try to justify principles philosophically. If there is nothing a priori true to be justified, Russell's philosophical problems have been solved (in essentials) and the questions themselves are logical misunderstandings concerning what is true and what lacks content. Indeed, the result of the *Tractatus* will be the bitter end of what Russell suggested in *Our Knowledge of the External World* happened with the question "Why?" in physics. There, he claims that if the question "means anything more than the search for a general law [. . .] then it is certainly the case that this question *cannot be answered* in physics *and ought not to be asked*" (Russell, 1914a: 227; my emphasis). Wittgenstein's point is that, in general, "if a question can be put at all, then it *can* also be answered" (TLP-OT: 6.5). Nevertheless, since "most propositions and questions, that have been written about philosophical matters, are not false, but senseless," we cannot answer these questions either (TLP-OT: 4.003). However, we can understand that the propositions that philosophers took as necessary (for instance, in science) do not say anything, but sometimes show formal structures.

In what follows, I show how Wittgenstein solves Russell's problems of philosophy and why he tells him in a letter written in March 1919, "I believe I've solved our problems finally" (WC: 89).

4.2 From Logic to Mathematics, and to Science

The fundamental point of TLP 6.1n is the final elucidation of the nature of logic by means of the characterization of its propositions as tautologies (TLP: 6.1). Tautologies show that propositions of logic have a "unique status among all propositions [*Sätze*]," for they are recognizable as true "from the symbol alone" (TLP: 6.112–3). That is, in the "suitable notation" of the book one recognizes the formal properties of such propositions by contrasting them with pictures (TLP: 6.122, 2.223–5). Of course, in truth tables one recognizes that pictures are contingently true and that "every tautology itself shows that it is a tautology" (TLP: 6.127) – see Section 3.5. One recognizes that a tautology is purely formal, empty of any content, and that necessity has nothing to do with any possible facts in the world. Contrary to Russell, logical laws have nothing to do with truths and "the fact that things behave in accordance with them" (Russell, 1912: 73).

The recognition of logical properties of sentences might also be presented in proofs in logic, in the derivations of tautologies from other tautologies. Therefore, contra Russell, there are no "self-evident logical principles" (Russell, 1912: 72). Primitive propositions in logic are just tautologies (TLP: 6.127). Therefore, there is no investigation of the grounds of logical evidence. The conclusion of TLP 6.1n is that "logic is transcendental," i.e., it is "not a body of doctrine [*keine Lehre*], but a mirror-image of the world" (TLP: 6.13). What is purely formal cannot be a doctrine or a theory, for what is formal does not say anything about the world.

One might see mathematical logic as composed of three different parts: a calculus of tautologies, a theory of identity, and a theory of classes. This approach is integral to the logicist program of reduction of mathematics to logic. The *Tractatus* makes clear that only the calculus of tautologies is pure logic, and that a theory of identity and a theory of classes are something else, something hypothetical that is dispensable in pure logic. Thus, although mathematics is a logical method, there is no logicist reduction (TLP: 6.2n).

We have seen that Russell's theory of identity introduced contingent elements, incompatible with the absolutely a priori character of logic (Section 2.5). The problem of contingency reappears in Russell's treatment of functions and classes. Essentially, by opposing variations of formalism, logicism's reduction of mathematics to logic presented a definition of numbers by means of classes. Without such a definition one could not explain the application of mathematics. Russell says, for instance, that without a definition of 'number,' '0,' and '1,' we could have "different interpretations" of those concepts, and thus would not be able to "apply mathematics," and it "would not suit daily life" (Russell, 1919: 9).

Different from the set-theoretical tradition in foundations of mathematics, Frege and Russell had an intensionalist conception of classes. Classes are always given by means of propositional functions (or concepts). Infinite classes can only be determined by propositional functions and any arbitrary class can be introduced by propositional functions. Suppose that Brown and Jones are the members of a class. Such a class, and any other class formed arbitrarily, can always be given by a common property, namely by the property "x is Brown or x is Jones," and so on. The idea of a property such as "being identical with x" is also the ground for Russell's definition of numbers, for equivalent classes are formed by means of propositional functions of the same form. Zero, for instance, is determined by a function $(x)\sim(x = x)$, which gives the class of things not identical with themselves, i.e., the empty class. It works similarly for the unit class, the class of couples, etc.

In his *Notebooks*, Wittgenstein refers to Russell's strategy to define numbers, and sees a fundamental problem:

> Isn't the Russellian definition of nought nonsensical? Can we speak of a class $\hat{x}$ $(x \neq x)$ at all? Can we speak of a class $\hat{x}$ $(x = x)$ either? For is $x \neq x$ or $x=x$ a function of x? Must not 0 be defined by means of the *hypothesis* $(\exists\varphi):(x)$ $\sim\varphi x$? And something analogous would hold for all numbers. (NB: 16)

In the *Tractatus*, the reference to the basic strategy of logicism appears in the following proposition:

> The theory of classes is completely superfluous in mathematics.
>   This is connected with the fact that the generality required in mathematics is not *accidental* generality. (TLP: 6.031)

Since classes are defined by propositional functions, which are true or false of objects, the logicist conception of numbers defined by classes is problematic. An accidental generality like $(\exists\varphi)(x) \sim\varphi x$, for instance, determines classes that are supposedly identical with numbers. Ultimately, the definition depends on hypotheses concerning how the world is. In this way, mathematics seems to depend on what is accidental, and the compulsion or necessity inherent to it seems to vanish. Thus, logicism distorts the essence of mathematics by introducing "accidental generality" as its ground instead of essential generality. If mathematics is known *a priori*, like logic, it cannot rely on propositional functions, which are true or false of objects when they determine classes.

This brings us to three other points: the elucidation that classes are superfluous for defining numbers, that mathematics is purely formal (essential generality), and that its application is guaranteed a priori. According to the *Tractatus*, classes are superfluous in mathematics because numbers are defined as exponents of the general form of an operation that works on the general form of propositions (TLP: 6.01).[48] Now, this is also meant to show how one can apply mathematics to the world. Numbers are applied to reality by means of complex sentences generated by the logical form of an operation that generates numbers. Since the operation that generates the logical complexity of sentences also generates the numbers, the application of numbers by means of sentences is guaranteed *a priori*.[49] The application takes place in ordinary sentences expressing mathematical inferences, grounded in mathematical equations operating as substitution rules (TLP: 6.2n and 6.0n, respectively; TLP: 6.211). In "real life," we *use* mathematical equations "*only* in inferences from propositions that do not belong to mathematics to others that likewise do not belong to

---

[48] For an account, see Marion (1998).

[49] For why it is important to guarantee a priori the application, see Frege (1903: §§91–3).

mathematics" (TLP: 6.211). This use shows that they are as empty of content as sentences of logic. They build a purely formal system of equations in which descriptions of facts can operate. Of course, "There are five apples on the table" is an empirical proposition, and not a proposition of mathematics. It is obviously contingent, accidentally true if true. Thus, the point is that application is grounded in equations that appear implicitly or explicitly in inferences, and not in cardinality or counting processes. Like logic, mathematics is not concerned with truth, but only with its possibility. Obviously, in logic we reason with possibilities: "*if* p is true and q is true, necessarily p and q are true." The same applies to mathematics: "*if* it is true that Brown has five apples, and it is true that Anna has 4, necessarily they have 9 apples together." As Wittgenstein says, "mathematics is a logical method" (TLP: 6.2).

Evidently, one should gather from all this that in essentials mathematics is purely formal, it does not say anything about the world or objects and its application is a priori certain in inferences. Consequently, *in essentials* there is no further question on foundations to be answered or anything true to be justified.

The group of remarks 6.3n, on science, begins with a result of the general form of a proposition: "outside logic everything is accidental" (TLP: 6.3). The major point here is that the general form also generates all "logical laws," which are the necessary laws (Section 3.4). Since mathematics is a "method of logic" (TLP: 6.234), outside logic and mathematics (both empty of content) everything is contingent.

With the discussion of science, thus, the concern is not any possible language as in mathematics and logic, for scientific theories and principles are not part of all possible languages. There are languages with no science, but no languages without pictures and tautologies. Yet, scientific theories have a formal function in our language. Theories are not direct descriptions of reality, but formal structures that unify true descriptions. They work like a net of certain pattern (triangles, squares, etc.) put over a sheet of paper with various figures on it that allows the description of each part of the paper according to the pattern of the net (TLP: 6.341). Thus, from a logical point of view, a theory is arbitrary, for we could use one of various possible nets and still have unified descriptions.[50]

One might think that this suggests that the *Tractatus* is simply introducing a pragmatist or instrumentalist view according to which science is 'true' to the extent that it works. However, this is not the Tractarian view. Descriptions of the

---

[50] Chapters 4 and 5 in Tejedor (2015) present a fresh perspective on Wittgenstein on scientific knowledge.

world are true or false, but a net, a scientific theory, is not. Each description put according to a net is independent from that net. This constitutes scientific evidence unified by a scientific net. In this way, true descriptions of the world that science must unify give us the objective basis on which science operates. Science must assemble true descriptions of the world, which are objectively independent.

The philosophically more relevant issue concerning science, according to Russell, is the justification or grounding of *Sätze* that are "principles of science," notably induction and causality. Those are indeed the major problems concerning science discussed in the *Tractatus*. For Russell, causality is expressed merely by general propositions that describe correlations between kinds of things. General propositions allow us "to infer the existence of one thing or event from another or of a number of others" (Russell, 1914a: 216). It is clear that correlations or laws, however, must be valid also in the future, and in order to infer the existence of one thing from the existence of another, we need, Russell says, "an a priori principle," which "is induction, not causality" (1914a: 226). Russell, therefore, claims that "if it [the principle of induction] is true, such inferences are valid, and if it is false, they are invalid" (1914a: 226). An a priori true principle of induction is therefore also essential for the justification of any single empirical statement about the future (Russell, 1912: 73). Otherwise, he claims, "we have no reason to expect that the sun will rise to-morrow" (1912: 68–9). Thus, one must accept the principle "on the ground of its intrinsic evidence" (Russell, 1912: 68).

According to the *Tractatus*, the induction principle neither is justified, nor justifies anything. It is not even an *a priori* principle. "Intrinsic evidence" is never useful anyway, for "if the truth of a proposition does not *follow* from the fact that it is self-evident to us, then its self-evidence in no way justifies our belief in its truth" (TLP: 5.1363). The proposition that seems to express the idea of induction, namely that sequences of events that happened in the past will also happen in the future is merely a "proposition with sense," i.e., it may be true or false (TLP: 6.31). Indeed, "it is an hypothesis that the sun will rise tomorrow" (TLP: 6.36311). We arrive at such hypotheses by means of what Wittgenstein calls a "procedure of induction" (TLP: 6.636). A procedure (*Vorgang*), in contrast to a principle grounding inferences, consists in *choosing* the simplest law. This, of course, is not a necessary step, and does not carry any logical compulsion. The compulsion behind the so-called a priori principles in science is purely psychological (TLP: 6.3631). It consists in the choice of the simplest form. To explain this might be a problem for psychology, but not a philosophical question to be decided a priori.

The law of causality is not necessary a priori either. Russell would agree that causality is not a necessary law of logic, but for Wittgenstein this means that there is no *a priori logical ground* for its acceptance, not even the principle of induction, as we have just seen. So we can understand the significance of the law of causality only if we look at its role or use in science, in its formal role in the symbolism of science, as it were. The "law of causality," Wittgenstein writes, "is not a law but the form of a law" (TLP: 6.32). The point here, I take it, is that the principle of causality itself is never stated in science and it is not an *explanation* or *ground* for a law of nature. We do not derive laws of nature from the law of causality. It is a formal restriction or rule used to build laws. It is assumed, for instance, in the very presentations of physical equations. Take, for instance, $f = m.a.$ The *form* of causality is shown in the fact that any change of numbers (effect) is explainable by means of the equation itself. If the force increases (effect), we say that the corresponding cause of change must be the increase of mass, and so on. If the equation, the law of nature, does not predict a fact correctly, and so fails to unify all true relevant propositions, we might say that the false prediction has an 'external' cause – say, the force of friction. We say that something caused the unexpected. In this case, we might need a law of friction with the form of causality, in accordance with other accepted laws. At worst, we replace the law itself or the theory of which it is part.

In any case, we do not give up the form of presentation of the law. If we find exceptions in a law with the form of causality, i.e., if the law does not unify all relevant true propositions, we fix the law or laws close to it, add a new law, etc. However, we never imply that the law of causality itself is wrong or false when things go wrong. Only what is formal is accepted no matter what takes place. Thus, the law is simply the formal means used to build the net of science. As Wittgenstein puts it, it is an a priori insight about the forms in which the laws of nature can be cast (TLP: 6.34).

However, the formality of causality is not *logically* necessary (it is not a tautology). The form of presentation of laws only shows that the form is an assumption. If there is any 'necessity' in the form in which we present 'laws of nature,' it is not because of logical compulsion. Therefore, the 'physical must' is deflated to a non-necessary form of scientific laws. The very form shows it, as in $f = m.a.$ Thus, it is needless to say it (TLP: 6.36).

Presumably, at this point problems concerning science and epistemology have been solved in essentials, since their formal a priori aspects have been elucidated. "Principles" are not truths that cannot be justified or falsified by experience. They are not truths at all, but empty of content, so that nothing at all known a priori philosophically as necessary justifies them.

4.3 From Logic to Ethics

In *Problems of Philosophy*, Russell claimed that there are "judgments of ethical or aesthetic value" (Russell, 1912: 117). One could almost say that "ethics and aesthetics are one" (TLP: 6.421). These judgments are "judgments as to what has *value on its own account*" that assert the "intrinsic desirability of things" (Russell, 1912: 76; my emphasis). He exemplifies the idea: "there are some self-evident ethical principles, such as 'we *ought* to pursue what is good' " (Russell, 1912: 112; my emphasis). Therefore, they must be true a priori principles: they "can be neither proved nor disproved by experience" (Russell, 1912: 76).

At this point, Russell is following Moore's conception of "pure judgments of intrinsic value" in *Principia Ethica* (Moore, 1903: 77).[51] In 'The Conception of Intrinsic Value,' written between 1914 and 1917, Moore further specifies his conception, perhaps having in mind conversations with Wittgenstein – they met in Norway in 1914. Neither generalization nor causality can account for the "intrinsic value" expressed in ethical principles, for something possesses intrinsic value only if it "would *necessarily* or *must* always, under all circumstances, possess it" (Moore, 1922: 265). Alternatively, it is *impossible* that it does not have the value. Therefore, only a proposition expressing necessary unconditional truth could be a proposition of ethics. However, Moore is unable to explain what is meant by this "unconditional 'must' " (Moore, 1922: 271).

From the logical point of view of the *Tractatus*, indeed, neither Russell nor Moore can explain the unconditional must of intrinsic value. Necessity is logical necessity (TLP: 6.3), which is seen in tautologies presented in truth tables. If *a priori* propositions of ethics (or aesthetics) were necessary and their negation impossible, they would simply lack content, as any 'intrinsically necessary' or 'unconditionally true' tautology and any impossible contradiction. The ethical-aesthetical-*must* would be, thus, empty. Of course, no particular value can be attached to an empty *Satz* of this kind. Certainly, as Moore and Russell thought themselves, the ethical-must is not derived from an empirical proposition either, since there would be no value in it: its conditional contingency and lack of enforcement would not characterize a 'must' (TLP: 6.422). Thus, no bipolar *Satz* would have a value either. One might well say, therefore, that all "*Sätze* are of equal value" (TLP: 6.4).

Thus, the very idea of finding ethical principles and justifying them should be abandoned. If one says, with Russell, "what is intrinsically of value is a priori *in the same sense* in which logic is a priori" (Russell, 1912: 76; my emphasis), then ethical propositions must be as empty as logical ones. Note that ethical principles cannot be derived *a priori* either, for, again, empty *a priori* propositions

---

51 See Engelmann (2016).

justify only other empty propositions (TLP: 6.126). Therefore, there is no grounding for ethical propositions. In the end, "Ethics is transcendental" (TLP: 6.421). This parallels "logic is transcendental" (TLP: 6.13). Logic is transcendental because it is not a theory or a "body of doctrine" (TLP: 6.13). Thus, since ethics is not a body of doctrine or theory either, there is no point in trying to justify or state ethical "principles" philosophically (TLP: 6.42). Of course, those would be at best empty tautologies anyway.

One might think, of course, that the ethical must/ought is a different kind of necessity, a different kind of compulsion (the compulsion of a legal law, for instance). Wittgenstein concedes this, but in this case, 'ought' must come with "something lending support and force to it" (WVC: 118; cf. TLP: 6.422). Without such a power, "Ought in itself is nonsensical" (WVC: 118). *Deus in absentia*, such a power is absent even in imagination in the modern scientific worldview.

4.4 Logic and Mysticism

Wittgenstein's Viennese background and his influences (Tolstoy, Kraus, and Weininger, for instance) are certainly central elements of the worldview underlying the *Tractatus*.[52] However, one should not think that the remarks on ethics and 'mysticism' primarily concern that background, as the "mystical reading" assumes (Section 1.1). Actually, as we will see, Wittgenstein principally uses the notion of 'mysticism' to deal with Russell's problems of philosophy. This explains why mysticism and skepticism appear together in TLP 6.5n.

An interesting biographical fact is that "a mystic illumination possessed" Russell in 1901 (Russell, 1968: 194). He had the feeling that "the loneliness of the human soul" can only be penetrated by "the sort of love that religious teachers have preached" (1968: 193–4). Although Russell's "mystic insight . . . largely faded," its effects persisted in many of his attitudes, particularly his pacifism during the First World War (1968: 194). It also appears in *The Free Man's Worship*, a paper from 1903 that Russell republished in *Philosophical Essays* and in *Mysticism and Logic*. There, religious resignation and its conquering of Fate is a characteristic of a "free man" who must preserve "a mind free from the wanton tyranny that rules his outward life" (Russell, 1910: 70). Russell's question was how the "mystical attitude," "impulse," "mood," or "feeling" was related to his 'scientific philosophy' (Russell, 1914a: 29, 56). His answer was that the "scientific attitude" *limits* what we

---

[52] For instance, TLP 6.52n express Tolstoian views. Wittgenstein's worldview and its connection with his influences is a complex issue, which goes beyond my goals here. See Engelmann (2016) for some discussion.

can know about ultimate reality, and so limits the aspirations of mysticism, but mysticism preserves the worship of beauty and truth in the inner life.

In 'The Limits of Philosophical Knowledge,' Chapter XIV of *Problems of Philosophy*, Russell criticizes philosophers who wanted to prove by "a priori metaphysical reasoning, such things as the fundamental dogmas of religion, the essential rationality of the universe, the illusoriness of matter, the unreality of evil, and so on" (Russell, 1912: 141). Nothing of the sort can be proved, since "we are unable to know the characters of the universe that are remote from our experience" (Russell, 1912: 145). Knowledge as to what exists is "limited to what we can know from experience" (Russell, 1912: 148). This means, for Russell, a "combination of experience with some wholly a priori principles, such as the principle of induction" (1912: 149). However, as seen in Section 2.2, ultimately all our knowledge is grounded in the "intuitive knowledge" of acquaintance with "hard data": sense-data, universals, and principles, according to various degrees of self-evidence (Russell, 1912: 149; 1914a: 77). A "logical experience" grounds Russell's logic. Thus, there is a tension in Russell's idea of 'limits of knowledge,' for his "hard data" reminds one of mystical "intuitive knowledge," in spite of his proviso that only sensation "supplies new data" (1914a: 36).[53]

Given the sensory limits of knowledge, according to Russell, philosophy can only pursue a "piecemeal investigation of the world" in agreement with the "scientific temper of our age" (Russell, 1912: 145). Supposedly, such a "humble" investigation recaptures the resignation of the religious or mystical attitude, since we must resign ourselves not to put forward doctrines about what lies "behind the veil" or beyond the world of the senses (Russell, 1914a: 70–1). Thus, philosophical investigation of Russell's scientific kind possesses "ethical neutrality" in the sense that it does not offer "a solution of the problem of human destiny, or of the destiny of the universe" (1914a: 28). The limits of philosophical knowledge, therefore, are the limits of our present conditions. The nature of what lies behind or beyond those limits is an unsolved, yet real problem.

In Russell's view, radical or "universal skepticism" shares a fundamental characteristic with 'mysticism,' and as such it is to be limited as well. Since universal skepticism is a consequence of hypotheses such as 'the evil genius' or 'the dream argument,' it leads to the claim of "the illusoriness of matter" (Russell, 1912: 18–22, 141). However, skepticism, unlike mysticism, does not claim any positive insight concerning a Reality behind or beyond experience. Russell's point against skepticism is that, since we do not have any "other source" of knowledge except the experience of sense-data, and since "all

---

[53] For a different account of Russell, Wittgenstein, and skepticism, see Diamond (2014).

refutation must begin with some piece of knowledge which disputants share," namely "hard" logic and sense-data, complete or universal skepticism is "unreasonable" (1912: 150).

Russell's argument against the skeptic is doubtful, since he also claims that experience is essentially "private" (1912: 19, 20, 28, 30). Thus, in *principle* "the kind of things which a man born blind *could never know* about the space of sight we also cannot know about physical space" (Russell, 1912: 32; my emphasis). Moreover, if logic depends on a "logical experience" (see Section 2.4), it can be subject to doubt. In this scenario, the sentence "universal skepticism, though logically irrefutable, is practically barren" (Russell, 1914a: 74) is no real consolation.

According to the *Tractatus*, "skepticism is *not* irrefutable, but obviously nonsensical, when it tries to raise doubts where no questions can be asked" (TLP: 6.51). Radical skepticism should disappear as a threat, for it is not irrefutable, but actually not a real problem at all. The "hard," true propositions of logic are simply tautologies, empty of any content, and thus *not subject to doubt* simply because they are not truths. Therefore, there is no question regarding the tautological truth of logic and, thus, no answer for a question either. Concerning the doubt about the very existence of the world, the "illusoriness of matter," it is also nonsense because the existence of the world is neither asserted nor denied by a meaningful proposition. There is no proposition to discuss in the case of radical skepticism. Of course, the "question" "Does the world exist?" could only make sense, as it were, if "The world exists" was already true, which is absurd. This would make sense depend on truth, and jeopardize logic itself (see Section 2.4). However, empty a priori logic cannot be jeopardized.

This brings us to mysticism. If it denies the existence of the world by claiming that everything is an illusion and that there is such and such a world behind or beyond the facts, it is as nonsensical as skepticism. A something beyond the facts ends up being just a fact anyway. However, contrary to what Russell thought, the "mystic" does not have to claim, and should not claim, such things. What one should realize is that the mystical feeling or attitude is not an expression of "how things are" in any possible world: "Not *how* the world is, is the mystical, but *that* it is" (TLP-OT: 6.44). "*That* the world is," however, contra Russell again, is not really the expression of an impossible experience lying beyond sensorial experience, simply because it is no expression of an experience at all. Actually, it expresses a 'tautologous' triviality that one understands when one does not distort, like Russell, the a priori character of logic:

> The 'experience' which we need to understand logic is not that such and such is the case, but that something *is*; but that is *no* experience.

> Logic precedes every experience – that something is *so*.
> It is before the How, not before the What. (TLP-OT: 5.552)

As we saw in Section 2.4, the need for an "experience" in logic is simply "out of the question" (NB, 3). *Any* world is in accordance with logic as expressed in the symbolism of the *Tractatus*. Contrary to Russell's understanding of logic, no How can be presupposed. After all, Wittgenstein eliminated the How presupposed by Russell's strange axioms of infinity and reducibility, and by his law of identity (Section 2.5). Thus, logic is before the How. However, any language has propositions with sense and names with meaning, which is "their connexion with the world" (TLP-OT: 6.124). This means that the logical symbolism expresses the connection with *any* world, any How. This is a *formal* What, which is shown in any proposition, since there is sense and there are named objects, whatever they are and their number (Section 2.6). It is a connection shown by any sentence at all making sense, not by a sentence being true.

What this reveals about logic and mysticism is that the logical symbolism recaptures formally "the inexpressible," the "mystical feeling," without strange "descriptions" and "experiences" of a Reality behind or beyond the world. Thus, in order to be a mystic, one does not need an experience beyond experience, which is an obvious piece of nonsense, but only a priori logic and what it shows: that there is something instead of nothing (TLP: 6.44, quoted above). Thus, Wittgenstein communicates indirectly that Russell himself could become a mystic again in these minimal terms, if he wished.

4.5 An Ethical Point After All

Echoing the preface, but also echoing what Russell had written about final explanations in science (quoted above), in TLP 6.5 Wittgenstein sums up TLP 6.n by pointing out that "*the riddle* does not exist" and that "if a question can be framed at all, it is also *possible* to answer it." Therefore, according to the correct logical point of view, no fundamental problem remains. However, a mystical feeling (TLP: 6.522, 6.45), an awe that the understanding of logic itself might make manifest, may remain, for one might feel unsatisfied even if all scientific questions are answered (TLP: 6.52). Scientific questions are answered by "what can be said" (TLP: 6.53), but they do not touch "the problems of life" (TLP: 6.52): they do not determine how or why one should live. As Russell said, perhaps in a Tolstoian mood, the world that science presents is "purposeless" and "void of meaning" (Russell, 1910: 60). According to Wittgenstein, propositions unified in science – conceived honestly – merely describe the world in accordance with one of various possible unifying theories and empty a priori formal principles (Section 4.2). Science itself, though not necessarily the philosophy of science, is ethically neutral. It will neither discover ethical views, nor justify ethical choices.

However, contrary to Russell, philosophical propositions cannot do that either (Sections 4.3–4.4). By means of his logical symbolism, and the elucidation of the symbolism in mathematics and science, Wittgenstein meant to communicate that the limits of language, of sense, show that philosophical propositions will not justify philosophical or scientific principles. Thus, answering what Russell considered central philosophical problems, namely the determination and grounding of the supposedly *true* necessary principles *a priori*, is a fruitless enterprise once we grasp the "logic of our language" and the purely formal character of principles.

Therefore, the ethical point of the book is that we should remain silent about all philosophical grounding of principles. This is, in a nutshell, the truth *communicated* in the book and referred to in its preface. Such a truth is not "rambling and roaring" and can be said in "three words," as the motto of the *Tractatus* suggests. Said directly, it means, "Whereof one cannot speak, thereof one must be silent" (TLP-OT: 7). From a logical point of view, to ground principles philosophically is simply to speak idle words, for it is at best a grounding of the groundless, the formal.

When Wittgenstein let his friend Hänsel read the manuscript of the *Tractatus*, he told him that it was the *logische Erledigung* (the logical finishing) of philosophy (Hänsel, 2012: 45). After Hänsel read it, Wittgenstein explained the ethical point that he himself took out of the book:

> His work is completed in the manuscript [TLP]. The question is solved: philosophy is silencing, the remainder is doing, [which] means: becoming a decent person. (Hänsel, 2012: 51; my translation)

"Doing" instead of saying idle words and "becoming a decent person" are, of course, ethical and religious notions untouched by science or philosophical grounding, and even less so by dogmas. However, the fact that ethical propositions have no ground does not mean that ethical views or teachings do not exist or should disappear. It means that the *choice* of ethical views or worldviews is not grounded philosophically. No sentence grounds something considered intrinsically valuable. Without grounding, the choice of an ethical view amounts to adopting it, living it, in contrast to trying to justify it by means of logic, science, philosophy, or dogmatic religious views.

For Wittgenstein *himself*, as he explains in his own words, living ethically boils down to becoming a decent person. This, for him, has a religious (Christian) motivation (Hänsel, 2012: 44–6). Since he talked about ethics on various occasions, one must suppose that engaging ethically may involve talking, but not, as he told the Vienna Circle, the "claptrap about ethics" of which he accused Moore (WVC: 69).[54] Talking about ethics is done in the first person, in a rather confessional tone: "all I can do is to step forth as an individual and speak in the first person" (WVC: 117).[55] Otherwise, one remains silent, giving up "grounding." For, contrary to Schopenhauer, "to preach morality is difficult, to ground morality impossible" (WVC: 118; modified translation). To preach morality is difficult, for one needs authority to do so; to ground morality is impossible, for ethical propositions would be empty, if necessary, and without compulsion, if contingent. Thus, one could say: "one should be able to stand by it without justification or explanation" (Engelmann 1967: 77). The unbiased eye sees that this is what really takes place after all.

---

[54] As Cahill put it, the *Tractatus* intends to remove at least one obstacle from a "transformation in life," namely "the illusion that a work consisting of philosophical sentences can show him how to live" (2011: 86).

[55] In his *Lecture on Ethics* from 1929, he talked about a "personal matter" (LE: 41). The confessional mode in particular ways of teaching ethics in a religion framework is characteristic of Tolstoy and Dostoevsky, who were, for Wittgenstein, certainly authoritative in such matters.

References

References

LC   D. Stern, B. Rogers and G. Citron, eds.*Wittgenstein: Lectures, Cambridge 1930–1933; From the Notes of G. E. Moore.* Cambridge: Cambridge University Press, 2016.

LE   A Lecture on Ethics. In *Philosophical Occasions, 1912–1951.* Edited by J. C. Klagge and A. Nordmann. Indianapolis: Hackett, 1993.

LO   *Letters to C. K. Ogden.* Oxford:Basil Blackwell, 1983.

NB   *Notebooks, 1914–1916.* 2nd edition. Translated by G. E. M. Anscombe. Chicago: The University of Chicago Press, 1979 [1961].

NL   Notes on Logic. In *Notebooks, 1914–1916.* 2nd edition. Translated by G. E. M. Anscombe. Chicago: The University of Chicago Press, 1979 [1961], pp. 93–107.

NM   Notes Dictated to Moore in Norway. In *Notebooks, 1914–1916.* 2nd edition. Translated by G. E. M. Anscombe. Chicago: The University of Chicago Press, 1979 [1961], pp. 108–119.

PI   *Philosophical Investigations.* 4th edition, revised. Edited by P. M. S. Hacker and J. Schulte, translated by G. E. M. Anscombe, P. M. S. Hacker and J. Schulte. Oxford: Wiley-Blackwell, 2009 [1953].

PPO   J. C. Klagge and A. Nordmann, eds. *Ludwig Wittgenstein: Public and Private Occasions.* New York: Rowman & Littlefield Publishers, 2003.

PT   *Prototractatus. Logisch-philosophische Abhandlung.* Kritische Edition. Edited by B. McGuinness and J. Schulte. Frankfurt: Suhrkamp, 2001.

RLF   Some Remarks on Logical Form. *Aristotelian Society,* Supplement 9 (1929), pp. 162–171.

TLP   *Tractatus Logico-philosophicus.* Translated by B. F. McGuinness and D. Pears. London: Routledge, 2004 [1961].

TLP-OT   *Tractatus Logico-Philosophicus.* Translated by C. K. Ogden, with an introduction by B. Russell. New York: Dover Publications, 1999 [1922].

WC   B. McGuiness, ed. *Wittgenstein in Cambridge: Letters and Documents, 1911–1951.* Oxford: Wiley-Blackwell, 2012.

WFL   B.McGuinness, ed. and P. Winslow, tr. *Wittgenstein's Family Letters*. London: Bloomsbury, 2018.

WVC   B. McGuinness, ed. and tr., J. Schulte, tr. *Wittgenstein and the Vienna Circle*. Oxford: Blackwell, 2003 [1979].

Anscombe, G. E. M. (1996 [1959]) *An Introduction to Wittgenstein's "Tractatus"*. Bristol: Thoemmes Press.

Bazzocchi, L. (2015) A Better Appraisal of Wittgenstein's *Tractatus* Manuscript. *Philosophical Investigations* 38:4, pp. 333–359.

Biletzki, A. (2003) *(Over)Interpreting Wittgenstein*. Dordrecht: Kluwer Academic Publishers.

Black, M. (1966) *A Companion to Wittgenstein's "Tractatus."* Ithaca: Cornell University Press.

Cahill, K. M. (2011) *The Fate of Wonder: Wittgenstein's Critique of Metaphysics and Modernity*. New York: Columbia University Press.

Carnap, R. (1959 [1934]) *The Logical Syntax of Language*. Translated by A. Smeathon. Paterson: Littlefield.

Conant, J. (1993) Kierkegaard, Wittgenstein and Nonsense. In T. Cohen, P. Guyer, and H. Putnam, eds., *Pursuits or Reason: Essays in Honor of Stanley Cavell*. Lubock, TX: Texas University Press, pp. 195–224.

(1995) Putting Two and Two Together: Kierkegaard, Wittgenstein and the Point of View for Their Works as Authors. In T. Tessin and M. von der Ruhr, eds., *Philosophy and the Grammar of Religious Belief*. New York: St. Martin's Press, pp. 248–331.

(2000) Elucidation and Nonsense in Frege and Early Wittgenstein. In A. Crary and R. Read, eds., *The New Wittgenstein*. London: Routledge, pp. 174–217.

(2005) What Ethics in the *Tractatus* is Not. In D. Z. Philips and M. von der Ruhr, eds., *Religion and Wittgenstein's Legacy*. London: Ashgate Publishing, pp. 39–95.

(2007) Mild Mono-Wittgensteinianism. In A. Crary, ed., *Wittgenstein and the Moral Life: Essays in Honor of Cora Diamond*. Cambridge, MA: MIT Press, pp. 31–142.

Conant, J. and Bronzo, S. (2017) Resolute Readings of the *Tractatus*. In H.-J. Glock and J. Hyman, eds., *A Companion to Wittgenstein*. Chichester: Wiley Blackwell, pp. 175–194.

Conant, J. and Diamond, C. (2004) On Reading the *Tractatus* Resolutely: Reply to Meredith Williams and Peter Sullivan. In M. Koelbel and B. Weiss, eds., *Wittgenstein's Lasting Significance*. London: Routledge, pp. 42–97.

Diamond, C. (1996) *The Realistic Spirit: Wittgenstein, Philosophy and the Mind*. Cambridge, MA: The MIT Press.

(2000) Ethics, Imagination and the Method of Wittgenstein's *Tractatus*. In A. Crary and R. Read, eds., *The New Wittgenstein*. London: Routledge, pp. 149–173.

(2004) Criss-Cross Philosophy. In E. Ammereller and E. Fischer, eds., *Wittgenstein at Work: Method in the "Philosophical Investigations."* London: Routledge, pp. 201–220.

(2014) The Hardness of the Soft: Wittgenstein's Early Thought about Skepticism. In J. Conant and A. Kern, eds., *Varieties of Skepticism: Essays after Kant, Wittgenstein, and Cavell*. Berlin: De Gruyter, pp. 145–182.

(2019) *Reading Wittgenstein with Anscombe: Going on to Ethics*. Cambridge, MA: Harvard University Press.

Engelmann, M. L. (2011) What Wittgenstein's 'Grammar' Is Not (On Garver, Baker and Hacker, and Hacker on Wittgenstein on 'Grammar'). *Wittgenstein-Studien* 2, 71–102.

(2013) *Wittgenstein's Philosophical Development: Phenomenology, Grammar, Method, and the Anthropological View*. Basingstoke: Palgrave Macmillan.

(2016) The Faces of Necessity, Perspicuous Representation, and the Irreligious "Cult of the Useful": The Spenglerian Background of the First Set of Remarks on Frazer. In L. Albinus and J. Rothhaupt, eds., *Wittgenstein's Remarks on Frazer: The Text and the Matter*. Berlin: De Gruyter, pp. 129–174.

(2017) What Does a Phenomenological Language Do? (Revisiting "Some Remarks on Logical Form" in Its Context). In M. Silva, ed., *Colours in Wittgenstein's Philosophical Development*. Basingstoke: Palgrave Macmillan, pp. 95–126.

(2018a) What Does it Take to Climb the Ladder? (A Sideways Approach). *Kriterion* 59:140, pp. 591–613.

(2018b) Instructions for Climbing the Ladder (The Minimalism of the *Tractatus*). *Philosophical Investigations* 41:4, pp. 446–470.

(2018c) Phenomenology in Grammar: Explicitation-Verificationism, Arbitrariness, and the Vienna Circle. In O. Kuusela, M. Ometita, and T. Ucan, eds., *Wittgenstein and Phenomenology*. London: Routledge, pp. 22–46.

Engelmann, P. (1967) *Letters from Ludwig Wittgenstein with a Memoir*. Edited by B. McGuinness and translated by L. Furtmuller. New York: Horizon Press.

Floyd, J. (2001) Numbers and Ascriptions of Numbers in Wittgenstein's *Tractatus*. In J. Floyd and S. Shieh, eds., *Future Pasts: The Analytic*

Tradition in Twentieth-Century Philosophy. Oxford: Oxford University Press, pp. 145–192.

Frege, G. (1987 [1884]) *Die Grundlagen der Arithmetik.* Stuttgart: Reclam.

(1962 [1903]) *Grundgesetze der Arithmetik (Begriffsschriftlich Abgeleitet) II.* Hildesheim: Georg Olms.

Goldfarb, W. (1997) Metaphysics and Nonsense: On Cora Diamond's *The Realistic Spirit. Journal of Philosophical Research* 22, pp. 57–73.

(2002) Wittgenstein's Understanding of Frege: The Pre-Tractarian Evidence. In E. Reck, ed., *From Frege to Wittgenstein.* Oxford: Oxford University Press, pp. 185–200.

Grasshoff, G. (1997) Hertzian Objects in Wittgenstein's Tractatus. *British Journal of the History of Philosophy* 5:1, pp. 87–119.

Hacker, P. M. S. (1986) *Insight and Illusion.* 2nd edition. Oxford: Clarendon Press.

(1999) Naming, Thinking and Meaning in the Tractatus. *Philosophical Investigations* 22:2, pp. 119–135.

(2000) Was He Trying to Whistle it? In A. Crary and R. Read, eds., *The New Wittgenstein.* London: Routledge, pp. 353–88.

Hänsel, L. (2012) *Begegnungen mit Wittgenstein – Ludwig Hänsels Tagebücher 1918–1919 und 1921–1922.* Edited by I. Somavilla. Wien: Haymon Verlag.

Hintikka, J. and Hintikka, M. (1986) *Investigating Wittgenstein.* Oxford: Blackwell.

Hutto, D. (2006) *Wittgenstein and the End of Philosophy: Neither Theory nor Therapy.* Basingstoke: Palgrave Macmillan.

Hylton, P. (1992) *Russell, Idealism, and the Emergence of Analytic Philosophy.* Oxford: Clarendon Press.

(2005) Logic in Russell's Logicism. In *Propositions, Functions, and Analysis.* Oxford: Oxford University Press, pp. 49–82.

Ishiguro, H. (1969) Use and Reference of Names. In P. Winch, ed., *Studies in the Philosophy of Wittgenstein.* London: Routledge, pp. 20–50.

Janik, A. and Toulmin, S. (1973) *Wittgenstein's Vienna.* New York: Touchstone.

Kierkegaard, S. (1974) *For Self-Examination and Judge for Yourself.* Translated by W. Lowrie. Princeton: Princeton University Press.

(1987) *Either/Or,* Part I. Translated by H. V. Hong and E. H. Hong. Princeton: Princeton University Press.

(2009a) *Concluding Unscientific Postscript to the Philosophical Crumbs.* Translated by A. Hannay. Cambridge: Cambridge University Press.

(2009b) *The Point of View for My Work as an Author.* Translated by H. V. Hong and E. H. Hong. Princeton: Princeton University Press.

Kremer, M. (1997) Contextualism and Holism in Early Wittgenstein: From *Prototractatus* to Tractatus. *Philosophical Topics* 25:2, pp. 87–120.

(2001) The Purpose of Tractarian Nonsense. *Nous* 35:1, pp. 39–73.

Kuusela, O. (2011) The Dialectic of Interpretations: Reading the *Tractatus*. In R. Read and M. A. Lavery, eds., *Beyond the "Tractatus" War: The New Wittgenstein Debate*. New York: Routledge, pp. 121–148.

(2019) *Wittgenstein on Logic and the Method of Philosophy*. Oxford: Oxford University Press.

Landini, G. (2007) *Wittgenstein's Apprenticeship with Russell*. Cambridge: Cambridge University Press.

Lugg, A. (2013) Wittgenstein's True Thoughts. *Nordic Wittgenstein Review* 2:1, pp. 33–56.

Malcolm, N. (1986) *Nothing is Hidden*. Oxford: Blackwell.

Marion, M. (1998) *Wittgenstein, Finitism, and the Foundations of Mathematics*. Oxford: Clarendon Press.

McGinn, M. (1999) Between Metaphysics and Nonsense: Elucidation in Wittgenstein's Tractatus. *Philosophical Quarterly* 49:147, pp. 491–513.

(2006) *Elucidating the "Tractatus."* Oxford: Clarendon Press.

McGuinness, B. (1988) *Wittgenstein: A Life; Young Ludwig (1889–1921)*. Duckworth.

(2002) *Approaches to Wittgenstein (Collected Papers)*. London: Routledge.

McManus, D. (2010) *The Enchantment of Words: Wittgenstein's "Tractatus Logico-philosophicus."* Oxford: Oxford University Press.

Moore, G. E. (2000 [1903]) *Principia Ethica*. Edited by T. Baldwin. Cambridge: Cambridge University Press.

(1922) The Conception of Intrinsic Value. In *Philosophical Studies*. New York: Kegan Paul.

Mounce, H. O. (1989) *Wittgenstein's "Tractatus": An Introduction*. Chicago: The University of Chicago Press, Midway Reprint Edition.

Moyal-Sharrock, D. (2007) The Good Sense of Nonsense. *Philosophy* 82, pp. 147–177.

Neurath, O. (1983 [1931a]) Physicalism. In *Philosophical Papers 1913–1946*. Dordrecht: D Reidel Publishing Company, pp. 52–57.

(1983 [1931b]) Sociology in the Framework of Physicalism. In *Philosophical Papers 1913–1946*. Dordrecht: D Reidel Publishing Company, pp. 58–90.

Pears, D. (1987) *The False Prison*, vol. 1. Oxford: Clarendon Press.

Potter, M. (2011) *Wittgenstein's Notes on Logic*. Oxford: Oxford University Press.

Rawls, J. (2001) *Justice as Fairness: A Restatement*. Edited by E. Kelly. Cambridge, MA: Harvard University Press.

Reid, L. (1998) Wittgenstein's Ladder: The *Tractatus* and Nonsense. *Philosophical Investigations* 212, pp. 97–151.

Rhees, R. (1996 [1970]) *Discussions of Wittgenstein*. Bristol: Toemmes Press.

Ricketts, T. (1996) Pictures, Logic, and the Limits of Sense in Wittgenstein's *Tractatus*. In D. Stern and H. Sluga, eds., *The Cambridge Companion to Wittgenstein*. Cambridge: Cambridge University Press, pp. 59–99.

(2014) Analysis, Independence, Simplicity, and the General Propositional-Form. *Philosophical Topics* 42:2, pp. 263–288.

Russell, B., (1992 [1905]) On Denoting. In *Logic and Knowledge*. London: Routledge, pp. 39–56.

(1910) *Philosophical Essays*. London: Longmans, Green, and Co.

(1997 [1912]) *The Problems of Philosophy*. Oxford: Oxford University Press.

(1999 [1913]) *Theory of Knowledge (The 1913 Manuscript)*. London: Routledge.

(1995 [1914a]) *Our Knowledge of the External World*. London: Routledge.

(2004 [1914b]) On Scientific Method in Philosophy. In *Mysticism and Logic*. New York: Dover Publications.

(1998a [1918]) *The Philosophy of Logical Atomism*. Chicago: Open Court.

(1998b [1919]) *Introduction to Mathematical Philosophy*. London: Routledge.

(1968) *The Autobiography of Bertrand Russell 1874–1914*. New York: Bantan Books.

(2002) *The Selected Letters of Bertrand Russell: The Public Years, 1914–1970*. Edited by N. Griffin. London: Routledge.

Russell, B. and Whitehead, A. N. (1973 [1910]) *Principia Mathematica (to *56)*. Cambridge: Cambridge University Press.

Stern, D. (2004) *Wittgenstein's "Philosophical Investigations": An Introduction*. Cambridge: Cambridge University Press.

Sullivan, P. (2004) What is the *Tractatus* About? In M. Koelbel and B. Weiss, eds., *Wittgenstein's Lasting Significance*. London: Routledge, pp. 28–41.

Tejedor, C. (2015) *The Early Wittgenstein on Metaphysics, Natural Science, Language, and Value*. New York: Routledge.

Von Wright, G. H. (1980) *Wittgenstein*. Minneapolis: University of Minnesota Press.

White, R. (2006) *Wittgenstein's "Tractatus Logico-Philosophicus."* London: Continuum.

Winch, P. (1987) *Trying to Make Sense*. Oxford: Basil Blackwell.

Acknowledgments

Thanks to CNPq (National Council for Scientific and Technological Development) for financial support. Thanks to IEAT-UFMG (Institute for Advanced Transdisciplinary Studies) for a partial leave of absence in 2017–8. Thanks to Anat Biletzki, Craig Fox, David Stern, João Cuter, Juliet Floyd, and Oskari Kuusela for comments on drafts of this Element. Thanks to Andrew Lugg, James Levine and Lynette Reid for a lively discussion of a draft of Section 2 at the online UEA Wittgenstein Workshop. I dedicate this work to Juliana.

Cambridge Elements ≡

The Philosophy of Ludwig Wittgenstein

David G. Stern

University of Iowa

David G. Stern is a Professor of Philosophy and a Collegiate Fellow in the College of Liberal Arts and Sciences at the University of Iowa. His research interests include history of analytic philosophy, philosophy of language, philosophy of mind, and philosophy of science. He is the author of *Wittgenstein's Philosophical Investigations: An Introduction* (Cambridge University Press, 2004) and *Wittgenstein on Mind and Language* (Oxford University Press, 1995), as well as more than 50 journal articles and book chapters. He is the editor of *Wittgenstein in the 1930s: Between the 'Tractatus' and the 'Investigations'* (Cambridge University Press, 2018) and is also a co-editor of the *Cambridge Companion to Wittgenstein* (Cambridge University Press, 2nd edition, 2018), *Wittgenstein: Lectures, Cambridge 1930–1933, from the Notes of G. E. Moore* (Cambridge University Press, 2016) and *Wittgenstein Reads Weininger* (Cambridge University Press, 2004).

About the Series

This series provides concise and structured introductions to all the central topics in the philosophy of Ludwig Wittgenstein. The Elements are written by distinguished senior scholars and bright junior scholars with relevant expertise, producing balanced and comprehensive coverage of the full range of Wittgenstein's thought.

Cambridge Elements ⹅

The Philosophy of Ludwig Wittgenstein

Elements in the Series

Printed in the United States
by Baker & Taylor Publisher Services